EVEREST

50 years of struggle to reach the top of the world

THIS IS A CARLTON BOOK

Text and Design copyright © 2002 Carlton Books Limited

This edition published by Carlton Books
An imprint of the Carlton Publishing Group 2002
20 Mortimer Street
London
W1T 3JW

A CIP catalogue for this book is available from the British Library.

ISBN 1 84222 838 2

Art Editor —Adam Wright
Design—Zoë Mercer
Production—Janette Burgin

Printed in Dubai

EVEREST

50 years of struggle to reach the top of the world

GEORGE CRAIG

Contents

introduction

It was in 1885 that author Clinton Dent first aired the possibility of climbing the highest mountain in the world, the one which had been named Everest after a former Surveyor General of India.

Although Tibet and Nepal were forbidden to explorers at this time and the elusive peak remained a distant vision through the Himalayan clouds, the challenge captured the imagination of the world's mountaineers, particularly the British. Over the next 68 years, political obstacles were overcome allowing 12 full-scale expeditions to attempt to conquer Everest. The first 11 ended in failure – and sometimes tragedy – until, finally, on 29 May 1953, the British team led by Colonel John Hunt achieved the seemingly impossible. Fittingly, news that Edmund Hillary and Sherpa Tenzing Norgay had made it to the summit of Everest

reached London on the day of the Coronation of Queen Elizabeth II. It gave the nation a reason for a double celebration.

The magic of Everest remains undiminished. Since 1953, over a thousand people – men and women, young and old, able bodied and climbers with disabilities – have conquered the mighty peak by a variety of different routes. Despite this it is still one of the world's supreme challenges, its very name synonymous with the biggest, the best and the most dangerous. Over 160 climbers have lost their lives in pursuit of their goal, some falling victim to avalanches, some to cold and exhaustion while others have simply disappeared off the face of the earth.

To celebrate the fiftieth anniversary of Hillary and Tenzing's epic ascent, this book chronicles the story of Everest and the characters that attempted the ultimate test of bravery. It recounts the great mysteries associated with the mountain – the disappearance of George Leigh Mallory and Andrew Comyn Irvine in 1924 and the sensational discovery of Mallory's body in 1999; Maurice Wilson, "the mad Yorkshireman", who launched an ill-fated solo expedition ten years later; Mick Burke who vanished near the summit in 1975; Joe Tasker and Peter Boardman who were last seen alive between the notorious Pinnacles in 1982; and of course, the riddle of the Abominable Snowman.

Above Lhotse and Everest shown from Makalu, Nepal.

the impossible dream?

At the start of the nineteenth century, the Andes were thought to be the highest mountains in the world. Western knowledge of the area around the Himalayas was distinctly sketchy until 1803 when British Captain Charles Crawford, reacting to requests for infantry officers to map any country they visited, conducted a survey of the "valley of Nepal" while he was posted in Kathmandu.

The following year, Crawford produced another map, this time of the whole of Nepal, which featured a line of distant peaks called the "snow mountains".

The Surveyor General of Bengal, Lieutenant. Colonel Robert Colebrook, was intrigued by Crawford's findings. He had already seen the snow-capped peaks from a distance of around 240 kilometres (150 miles) and resolved to take a closer look. Temporarily winning over the ruler of Nepal, who habitually refused to allow strangers to enter the country, Colebrook set out to explore the sources of the Ganges, only to be taken ill shortly before the expedition was due to depart. His place was taken by a young lieutenant, W.S. Webb, who, in 1810, calculated some of the "snow mountain" peaks to be in excess of 7,925 m (26,000 ft) – a figure that would make them the highest mountains in the world. However, geographers outside India dismissed Webb's claims and continued to hail the Andes as the summit of the earth.

Above **Mount Everest in the Himalayas – the highest mountain in the world.**

First Western Sighting

Meanwhile in 1808, the British India Survey began the task of producing reliable maps of the entire Indian sub-continent. It was an onerous mission and, starting at the southern tip of India and working their way north, it took them 30 years to reach the Himalayas, their progress slowed by huge surveying theodolites, which were so heavy a dozen men were needed to carry each one. And when they finally reached Nepal, they found the way barred, necessitating their work to be carried out from remote observation stations. In 1847, the Surveyor General, Andrew Waugh, spotted a snow-covered peak some 224 kilometres (140 miles) beyond Kangchenjunga, which until then had been thought to be the highest in the range. The new mountain became known as Peak XV (each was given a number) and in 1856, as a result of closer surveys, Waugh was finally able to put its height at 8,840 m (29,002 ft), nearly 305 m (1,000 ft) higher than Kangchenjunga. Waugh concluded that Peak XV was "most probably the highest in the world".

Above **Andrew Waugh.**
Right **Sir George Everest.**

Waugh's figure was accepted as the official height until the 1950s when Indian surveyors, from much closer vantage points, calculated the summit to be 8,848 m (29,028 ft). In the meantime, of course, the world's highest mountain had acquired a name. For Waugh decided to name it after his predecessor as Surveyor General of India – George Everest. Despite objections by Everest himself who insisted that the peak should be given a local name, "Everest" was officially adopted by the Royal Geographical Society (RGS) 1865, just one year before George Everest died.

Above Mount Everest range
from Vandakphu 1890–1900.

Left Map of Tibet at the turn
of the century.

Twenty years later, in his book *Above the Snowline*, Clinton Dent became the first person to suggest publicly that it might be possible to climb Everest, although he did concede that it might not necessarily be wise to do so. The idea grew in popularity and Gurkha officer the Hon. Charles Bruce suggested to Colonel Francis Younghusband, who was to lead a mission to Tibet, that they should cross Tibet and climb Everest. The prospect appealed to Younghusband and, on a reconnaissance trip into western Tibet, two of his officers got close enough to Everest from the north to decide that the north ridge offered the best route of ascent. However, the British government refused to submit a request to Tibet for permission to climb so that the only westerner to venture close to Everest was intrepid Englishman Captain John Noel who, in 1913, his skin and hair darkened to make him look like a local, made an illegal incursion to within 96 kilometres (60 miles) of the great peak.

First Recce

The First World War prevented any similar forays but Francis Younghusband's elevation to the post of President of the Royal Geographical Society, coupled with a captivating lecture to the society from Captain Noel, created renewed enthusiasm. Having obtained the approval of the British, Indian and Tibetan governments, the RGS and the Alpine Club formed an Everest Committee in January 1921, the aim being to send an eight-man expedition to find a route up Everest with a view to despatching a full-scale expedition the following year. Bruce was the obvious choice of leader but prior military engagements meant that the honour was passed to Lieutenant Colonel Charles Howard-Bury who had played a key role in the diplomatic negotiations with the various governments.

No sooner had the party left Darjeeling in May 1921, than they encountered their first problems. The terrain was unforgiving and the climate, a combination of heat and dusty winds in

Left Intrepid explorer Captain Noel whose enthusiasm rekindled interest in conquering Everest.

Below Preliminary map of Mount Everest constructed at the RGS from photographs and sketches from the 1921 expedition.

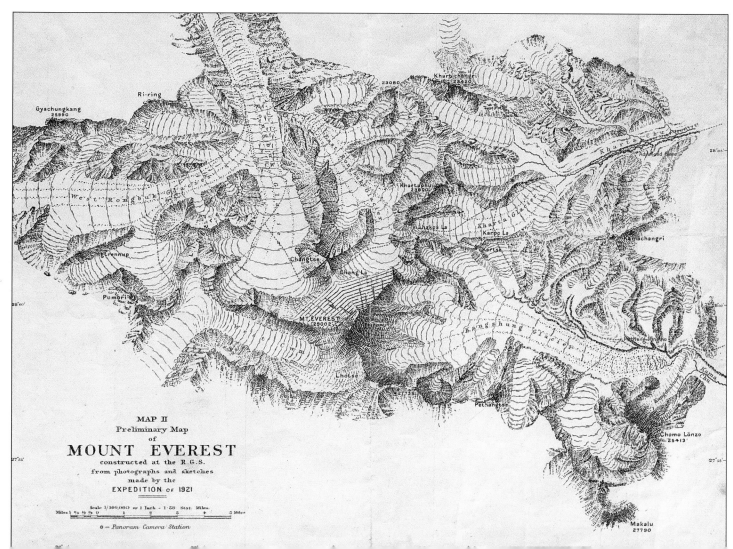

MAP II
Preliminary Map
of
MOUNT EVEREST
constructed at the R.G.S.
from photographs and sketches
made by the
EXPEDITION of 1921

Scale 1/100,000 or 1 Inch = 1.58 Stat. Miles.

o = Panoram Camera Station

the morning and bitter cold at night, sapped everyone's energy. The army mules that were carrying the equipment proved woefully inadequate and were replaced by hill mules and yak. The senior doctor, Alexander Kellas, died of heart failure and the atmosphere between former schoolmaster George Mallory and Howard-Bury was chillier than the Himalayan nights. However, they pressed onwards and, on 13 June, Mallory climbed a steep cliff in the hope of catching his first view of Everest through the clouds. He wrote:

> Presently the miracle happened. A whole group of mountains began to appear in gigantic fragments ... like the wildest creation of a dream. A preposterous triangular lump rose out of the depths; its edge came leaping up at an angle of about 70 degrees and ended nowhere. To its left a black serrated crest was hanging in the sky incredibly. Gradually, very gradually, we saw the great mountainsides and glaciers and arêtes ... until far higher in the sky than imagination had dared to suggest the white summit of Everest appeared.

Together with Guy Bullock, Mallory explored the Rongbuk and West Rongbuk glaciers that lead to the north face of Everest, climbing to heights of over 6,100 m (20,000 ft). The western ridge and the east face were also examined from various vantage points but were deemed inaccessible. Convinced that the key to the ascent of Everest lay in reaching the North Col at the summit of the glaciers on Everest's north-east ridge, the expedition climbed the Lhakpa La, a pass at the head of the Kharta valley, from where they were able to see an easy descent to the East Rongbuk glacier, newly discovered by the party's photographic assistant, Major E. Oliver Wheeler. The East Rongbuk led directly on to the North Col although it was by no means an easy climb. Bad weather hindered progress but on 24 September, Mallory, Bullock and Wheeler finally reached the North Col at almost 7,010 m (23,000 ft). Mallory contemplated a push for the summit itself but fatigue and fearful blizzards forced a retreat. Even so, they descended to camp, certain that they had unlocked the secret of the route to the top.

Right **Base Camp Everest** 1921.

The 1922 Expedition – First Loss of Life

Optimism ran high as preparations began for the 1922 assault on Everest, although Mallory sounded a cautionary note. "We must remember," he wrote, "that the highest of mountains is capable of severity, a severity so awful and so fatal that the wiser sort of men will do well to think and tremble even on the threshold of their high endeavour."

The expedition was led by the experienced General Charles Bruce who established base near the Rongbuk glacier before the end of April to beat the monsoon season, which began around the middle of June. At 56, he planned to leave the assault on the summit to younger men – Mallory, Edward Norton, Dr. Howard Somervell and Australian George Finch. But when, on 16

Below **Captain Noel**
cinematographing the ascent
of Everest from Chang La.

May, clouds bubbled up ominously to threaten an early monsoon and Finch was delayed at base camp with stomach pains, his place was taken by 40-year-old Colonel H.T. Morshead. On the 17 May, this quartet climbed to the North Col, assisted by ten Sherpas, the local people who not only served as porters, but were also natural mountaineers. Bruce had originally planned to pitch two camps above the North Col, in line with Mallory's insistence that the final assault should start from no lower than 8,230 m (27,000 ft), but a lack of porters necessitated the sacrifice of one camp. It was therefore hoped to make the final push from somewhere in excess of 7,925 m (26,000 ft).

On the morning of 20 May, over half of the porters were indisposed from altitude-sickness. The remainder of the party set off from Camp IV on the North Col at 6,980 m (22,900 ft), but by 12.30 p.m. they had encountered biting winds and were forced to establish Camp V at 7,620 m (25,000 ft). Mallory's finger-tips and Norton's ears had succumbed to frostbite, but worst hit of all was Morshead whose fingers and toes were in a bad way. So when the team started out for the summit at eight o'clock the following morning, Morshead turned back almost at once. The others reached 8,170 m (26,800 ft) before admitting defeat. Tragedy nearly struck on the way down when one of the climbers slipped and dragged two others off the ridge.

Above **Mallory and Norton climbing at 8,169 m (26,800 ft) in 1922.**

Left **Camp on Everest 1922, photo taken by Captain Finch.**

Instinctively, the lead climber, Mallory, rammed the pick of his axe deep into the snow, wound the rope around its head and threw the whole of his weight on to the axe to hold it down. Somehow the pick and the rope held the three fallen men and disaster was averted thanks to Mallory's quick thinking.

On the way down, they passed George Finch and the novice Geoffrey Bruce who were trying out the oxygen apparatus in preparation for the second assault. There were mixed feelings about using additional oxygen in Everest's rarefied air. Some found it an invaluable aid while others considered it to be cheating and thought the equipment itself was so cumbersome as to be more of a hindrance than a help. But Finch and Bruce were able to reach 8,320 m (27,300 ft) with oxygen before Bruce's supply suddenly failed. Finch quickly connected his supply to Bruce and carried out on-the-spot repairs but the effects of having been forced by fearsome gales to spend two nights at high altitude with little food had taken their toll. The two men turned back and tucked in to a welcome meal of tinned quails truffled in pâté de foie gras at Base Camp.

By 3 June, Mallory, Finch and Somervell had rested sufficiently to contemplate a third attempt even though there were further indications of an early monsoon. Finch soon realized the effort was beyond him but the others, joined by Arthur Wakefield and Colin Crawford, forged ahead to Camp III at 6,400 m (21,000 ft), below the slopes of the North Col. At 8 a.m. on 7 June, the party, plus 13 Sherpas, set off from Camp III but at some 180 m (600 ft) below the crest of the North Col, Mallory heard what he later described as:

Below George Finch testing the early oxygen equipment.

a noise not unlike an explosion of untamped gunpowder. I had never before been near an avalanche of snow, but I knew the meaning of that noise as though I were accustomed to hear it every day. In a moment I observed the snow's surface broken only a few yards away to the right and instinctively moved in that direction. And then I was moving downward. Somehow I managed to turn out from the slope so as to avoid being pushed headlong and backwards down it … Then the rope at my waist tightened and held me back. A wave of snow came over me. I supposed that the matter was settled. However, I thrust out my arms to keep them above the snow and at the same time tried to raise my back, with the result that, when after a few seconds the motion stopped, I felt little pressure from the snow and found myself on the surface.

Although the British climbers survived, the sudden avalanche had swept seven Sherpas to their deaths. The monsoon had indeed arrived and the assault was abandoned. Everest had claimed its first victims.

The 1924 Expedition – The Disappearance

George Leigh Mallory was the golden boy of British mountaineering. Born on 18 June 1886 in Mobberley, Cheshire, the son of a clergyman, he was by all accounts a fearless child. At the age of seven he was sent to his room for misbehaving during teatime, only for his family to discover him climbing the roof of the adjoining church. "I did go to my room," he argued, "to fetch my cap!" One of his two sisters (he also had a brother, Trafford) once recalled:

> It was always fun doing things with George. He had a knack of making things exciting and often rather dangerous. He climbed everything that it was possible to climb. I learnt very early that it was fatal to tell him that any tree was impossible for him to get up.

Educated at Winchester (where he excelled in sporting rather than academic matters) and Cambridge, he briefly considered joining the church before finally opting for a post as assistant master at Charterhouse School on an annual salary of £270. It was there that he met Ruth Turner, the daughter of a local architect, and following a whirlwind romance the pair were married in 1914. With Britain at war, the newlyweds had to abandon their plans for an Alpine honeymoon in favour of a camping holiday in the West Country, where their lifestyle under canvas aroused such mistrust among the locals that they were arrested on suspicion of being German spies!

After serving as a gunner in the First World War, in 1923 Mallory started a new job in Cambridge teaching adults instead of children, a switch which he found immensely rewarding. By then he and Ruth had three small children. Yet their periods apart had become all too frequent – initially on account of the war but latterly to accommodate Mallory's craving for adventure.

Mallory's philosophy was simple. "To refuse the adventure," he once said, "is to run the risk of drying up like a pea in its shell." He first took up climbing at Winchester and went to the Alps at the age of 18. University holidays were spent climbing in Wales and the Lake District where he perfected the techniques that were to stand him in good stead on higher peaks. His bravery was unquestionable, as was his charisma, although his friend, Geoffrey Young, once warned him: "Your weakness, if any, is that you … do not hold back from allowing yourself to sweep weaker brethren, carried away by their belief in you, to take risks or exertions that they were not fit for."

Mallory also displayed an alarming tendency for absent-mindedness. He had been known to forget to "rope up" before attempting a tricky Alpine ascent, prompting General Charles Bruce to remark: "He is a great dear, but forgets his boots on all occasions." An experienced Austrian mountaineer, led by Mallory up a difficult route in Wales, took a more sinister view of his mix of impulsiveness and forgetfulness, commenting ominously: "That young man will not be alive for long!"

At 5ft 11in tall and weighing 159lb, Mallory was a supreme athlete. His one handicap was a tender right ankle, the legacy of a characteristic act of foolhardiness. Back in 1909 he was out walking with his sisters and friends near his parents' home on the Wirral when he arrived at a small sandstone cliff in a disused quarry. Unable to resist the challenge of climbing it, he launched himself into the ascent with typical gusto, only to run into unexpected difficulties. Attempting to

Above **George Mallory, the golden boy of British mountaineering.**

extricate himself with a flying dismount on to the grass below, he instead landed hard with his right foot on a hidden stone. He assumed that he had merely sprained his ankle, but it refused to heal. It was only eight years later, when it caused him so much pain that he had to be invalided home from the Great War, that he learned that he had broken the ankle in the 1909 fall. He underwent an operation to repair the damage but the injury was still troubling him on the 1924 expedition. From Darjeeling in May of that year, he wrote to Ruth: "The only doubts I have are whether the old ankle one way or another will cause me trouble."

The great challenge to any mountaineer in the years following the Great War was to conquer Everest. Mallory became obsessed with this goal and was a member of the first three expeditions to tackle the peak. He was in the parties that were the first to see the North Face and to reach the North Col. He was also the first to see the Western Cwm, from where the eventual triumph of 1953 was gained, although Mallory himself considered it impracticable.

Below **The ill-fated Mount Everest expedition of 1924. Left to right: (standing) Irvine, Mallory, Norton, Odell and Macdonald; (seated) Shebeare, Bruce, Somervell and Beetham.**

But on that third expedition, in 1924, Mallory became the central figure in a mystery over which controversy still rages.

Mallory was curiously reluctant to join the 1924 expedition. He was settled in his new job and wary of being parted from his family yet again. Besides which he still felt guilty over the loss of the Sherpas in 1922 – "brave men" whom he felt were "ignorant of mountain dangers, like children in our care." Whilst he had not been publicly criticized for choosing to traverse the North Col so soon after fresh snow, there were private mutterings that his actions had bordered on the reckless and that they had contributed to the deaths of the hapless porters. Mallory himself accepted his share of blame, musing: "More experience, more knowledge might perhaps have warned us not to go there. One can never know enough about snow."

In the end he just about overcame his misgivings. "It would look rather grim," he wrote to his father, "to see others, without me, engaged in conquering the summit … I have to look at it from the point of view of loyalty to the expedition and of carrying through a task begun." The lure of Everest, it seemed, was too powerful to resist although he did confide to an old Cambridge friend, Geoffrey Keynes, that he had grave doubts as to whether he would ever return from the mountain. "This is going to be more like war than mountaineering," said Mallory frankly. "I don't expect to come back."

Even on the voyage east, it was evident that Mallory was in a state of torment, his heart split between Everest and Ruth. He acknowledged this in a letter to her dated 8 March 1924 in which he wrote:

> I fear I don't make you very happy. Life has too often been a burden to you lately, and it is horrid when we don't get more time and talk together…Somehow or another, we must contrive to manage differently – to have some first charge upon available time for our life together.

Preparing for the Summit

The 1924 expedition was to be led by General Charles Bruce but he was struck down by malaria in the early stages of the gruelling trek across Tibet and Major Edward Norton took his place. Mallory was appointed climbing leader and immediately began devising plans for reaching the summit. In a letter of 17 April he informed Ruth of his "brain-wave". Two men, with some 15 porters, would climb from Camp IV on the North Col to Camp V, build four tent platforms at around 7,770m (25,500ft) and descend. Another pair – the first "gasless" summit party – would occupy Camp V one night before pushing on with eight porters, missing out Camp VI, to establish a Camp VII at 8,320m (27,300ft). At the same time the second summit party – using oxygen – were to establish Camp VI at 8,077m (26,500ft). "Then," concluded Mallory, "the two parties start next morning and presumably meet on the summit."

Norton was suitably impressed by the plan but in the event Mallory's vision of a Camp VII perched precariously on the north-east ridge, some 550m (1,700ft) below the summit, never materialized.

The preparation of what he deemed to be a practical plan seemed to lighten Mallory's mood and on 24 April he wrote to Ruth in more optimistic tones, ending:

On May 17th or thereabouts we should reach the summit…The telegram announcing our success, if we succeed, will precede this letter, I suppose; but it will mention no names. How you will hope that I was one of the conquerors! And I don't think you'll be disappointed.

Six days later – on 30 April – the party arrived at the Rongbuk Base Camp at the height of a raging blizzard. In a letter to his sister Mary, Mallory remarked that the prevailing conditions looked "most unpleasant for climbing", adding that he was determined to avoid a repeat of the tragedy of 1922. "No one," he wrote, "climber or porter, is going to get killed if I can help it. That would spoil all."

There was a grim reminder of the dangers that lay ahead when Camp III was engulfed in a fierce blizzard. The atrocious May weather delayed the expedition by two weeks and once more the spectre of an early monsoon – the bane of 1922 – loomed large.

Finally on 20 May – three days after he had envisaged setting foot on the summit – Mallory led a four-man party on to the North Col, only to plunge into a hidden crevasse when descending to Camp III via the ill-starred 1922 route. Writing to Ruth, he recounted:

Below A fierce blizzard severely hampered progress from Camp III.

The snow gave way, and in I went with the snow tumbling all round me, down luckily only about ten feet before I fetched up half-blind and breathless to find myself most precariously supported only by my ice-axe, somehow caught across the crevasse and still held in my right hand – and below was a very unpleasant black hole.

Mallory shouted to his colleagues for help but his calls went unanswered. Eventually he managed to extricate himself from his predicament and negotiate a tricky path to safety but by the time he was reunited with the others Mallory admitted that this latest setback had "just about brought me to my limit".

Worse was to follow. The next day the quiet man of the party – John de Vere Hazard – waited at Camp IV with 12 porters in readiness for the arrival of Geoffrey Bruce and Noel Odell who were intending to use the porters to establish Camp V. However a prolonged snowstorm left Bruce and Odell stranded at Camp III and on the 23 May Hazard decided to come down. He reached Camp III at 5pm, but with only eight of the 12 porters. Mallory was livid. He wrote:

It is difficult to make out exactly how it happened, but evidently he didn't shepherd his party properly at all, and in the end four stayed up, and one of these badly frostbitten.

On 24 May, Somervell, Norton and Mallory set off to rescue the four lost porters. Mallory was very much the driving force and, with a combination of gentle encouragement allied to sheer brute force, the four porters were eventually coaxed back down the mountain. But it was dark when they arrived back at Camp III and the sorry episode did little to boost morale.

The treacherous weather showed no signs of abating. Not surprisingly the Sherpas had become fearful and after 24 May only 15 of the 55 porters were able – or willing – to work above Camp III. The party was in such a state of despair and disarray that Norton ordered a mass retreat and by 25 May the team had limped all the way down to Camp I. Two days later Mallory, who by now had fallen victim to a racking cough, wrote what turned out to be the last letter Ruth would ever receive from him: "It has been a bad time altogether. I look back on tremendous effort and exhaustion and dismal looking out of a tent door into a world of snow and vanishing hopes."

Just when everything appeared lost, the weather relented at last and the climbers regained the high ground. The first attempt on the summit was made on 1 June by Mallory and Geoffrey Bruce, who established Camp V at 7,710 m (25,300 ft) on the north ridge. Mallory was ready to push on the following morning but Bruce was too exhausted and, with the porters also severely weakened, there was no choice but to head back down to Camp IV.

The second attempt was made by Norton and Somervell. The latter, a literary buff who used to read Shakespeare to Mallory in his tent, was troubled by a throat infection and had to make numerous stops to get his breath. "Our pace was wretched," admitted Norton, who set himself a target of taking 20 steps without a rest, but never bettered 13. "We must have looked a very sorry couple."

Above **Mallory and Irvine leaving the North Col on that fateful last climb.**

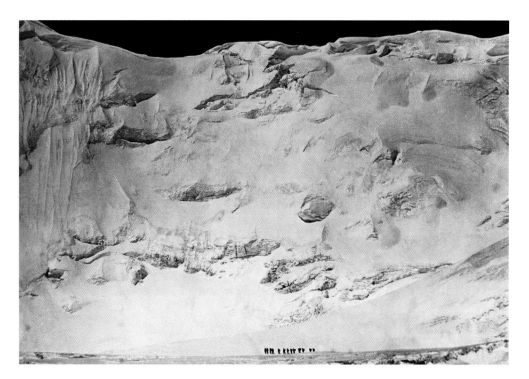

Eventually at noon on 4 June, at around 8,445 m (27,700 ft), a distraught Somervell could face no more and told Norton to continue alone. The weather was now fine and Norton forged ahead. He became the first person to reach the great gully, or couloir, which leads up the side of the summit pyramid (it was later named the Norton Couloir in his honour) but, after an hour on his own, found its steep rocks too hazardous for a single climber to negotiate. He was also suffering from double vision, having made the mistake of removing his goggles while on rock. He later wrote:

I found myself stepping from tile to tile, as it were, each tile sloping smoothly and steeply downwards; I began to feel that I was too much dependent on the mere friction of a boot nail on the slabs. It was not exactly difficult going, but it was a dangerous place for a single unroped climber, as one slip would have sent me in all probability to the bottom of the mountain. The strain of climbing so carefully was beginning to tell and I was getting exhausted. In addition my eye trouble was getting worse and was by now a severe handicap.

At a record height of 8,573 m (28,126 ft), Norton turned back. Unless Mallory and Irvine surpassed that height four days later, his altitude record would stand for 29 years until overtaken by Hillary and Tenzing. At any rate Norton's feat of reaching that height without supplementary oxygen lasted until 1978 when Peter Habeler and Reinhold Messner attained the summit without gas.

Realizing that they could not possibly reach the top before midnight and would probably freeze to death if they proceeded, Norton and Somervell opted to return to Camp IV. Somervell very nearly didn't make it, lapsing into a frightening coughing fit, relieved only by an eruption of blood and mucus. It later emerged that he had coughed up the lining of his larynx. As Norton staggered towards camp in the gathering gloom, one of the meeting party announced that he was coming up with an oxygen cylinder. "We don't want the damned oxygen," replied Norton, summoning his last ounce of energy. "We want drink!" In his book, *After Everest*, Somervell reflected on their predicament.

We had been willing always to risk our lives, but we did not believe in throwing them away, so we decided that we must go down the mountain and own ourselves beaten in fair fight. No fresh snow, no blizzards, no intense cold had driven us off the peak. We were just two frail mortals, and the biggest task Nature has yet set to man was too much for us.

The Third Attempt

Four days later, early on the morning of 8 June, Mallory set off for the third attempt on the summit. He had been expected to choose as his partner the experienced geologist Noel Odell but instead selected 22-year-old undergraduate Andrew Comyn Irvine. The youngest and by far the least experienced member of the expedition, Irvine, known as "Sandy" because of his blond hair and fair complexion – a trait that left him prone to serious sunburn in Tibet – had already twice represented Oxford University in the Boat Race and was also a "Blue" at squash. His surprise inclusion in the 1924 Everest party owed everything to a meeting with Odell in Spitzbergen, Norway, the previous summer. Odell was impressed by Irvine's mental and physical toughness and enduring good humour and consequently, although he had yet to climb higher than 1,830m (6,000ft), the young man from Birkenhead was added to the expedition.

Irvine's ability to mend almost anything mechanical quickly made him invaluable. Somervell wrote: "If ever a Primus-stove goes wrong, it goes straight to Irvine, whose tent is like a tinker's shop." Mallory's first impressions of the newcomer were equally favourable. In one of his letters to Ruth he wrote of Irvine: "sensible and not highly strung he'll be one to depend on, for everything perhaps except conversation." However Mallory did subsequently qualify his praise by confiding: "Against him is his youth – hard things seem to hit him a bit harder – and his lack of mountain training and practice which must tell to some extent when it comes to climbing rocks or even to saving energy on the easiest ground."

Above **Andrew Irvine.**

Below **Noel Odell, the last person to see Mallory and Irvine alive.**

Mallory decided to opt for Irvine principally for his expertise with the heavy oxygen equipment that they would be carrying. Norton urged him to take Odell instead but, still suffering from snow-blindness and in considerable discomfort, was reluctant to overrule the man he had appointed as climbing leader. Thus Mallory and Irvine left Camp VI at 8,170 m (26,800 ft) in one last attempt to reach the summit. In a final note to Odell, Mallory apologized for leaving the camp in a mess and declared that the oxygen was "a bloody load for climbing" but that they had "perfect weather for the job."

Odell was climbing in support of Mallory and Irvine that morning. At some 610 m (2,000 ft) below the pair, he had seen nothing of them since leaving Camp V and during mid-morning, clouds drifted across their route on the north-east ridge, rendering observation impossible. Then suddenly at 12.50 p.m., the clouds broke, enabling Odell to glimpse them in the distance. In a dispatch to *The Times*, he wrote:

> The entire summit ridge and final peak of Everest were
> unveiled. My eyes became fixed on one tiny black spot
> silhouetted on a small snow-crest beneath a rock step in

Look Out for the
WEMBLEY GUIDE
With the Blue Cover.

What to see and how to find it. A one day tour. How to get there. The amusements. Where to dine. What the children like. "Where is it" Index. Photographs and SIX MAPS.

BOOKSTALLS & **1/-** NEWSAGENTS

BY POST 1/1½, from "Daily News" Publications Department, Bouverie St., E.C.4.

Daily News

FINAL EDITION

JUST OUT.
LAWN T

No. 24418.   LONDON, THURSDAY, JUNE 26, 1924.   ONE PENNY.

HOW MALLORY AND IRVINE PERISHED.

HEROISM ON MOUNT EVEREST.

DEATH WHILE "GOING STRONG FOR THE TOP."

ALL RECORDS BROKEN.

GREAT STORY OF LAST ASSAULT ON SUMMIT.

"When last seen Mallory and Irvine were going strong for the top."

So says Lieut.-Col. Norton, the leader of the Mount Everest expedition, in a message sent on June 11, immediately after the two climbers had met their death, as already recorded.

In other messages, dispatched apparently only two days before the disaster, and the abandonment of the assault on the summit, it is disclosed that Mr. Mallory and Mr. Irvine reached a height of 28,000 feet, beating all Everest records. Mount Everest is 29,000 feet high, so the two dead climbers got to within 1,000 feet of the top.

HEROIC ENDURANCE.

"Beaten By Shortness of Breath."

From Lieut.-Colonel E. F. NORTON.

CAMP THREE (21,000ft.), EAST RONG-BUK GLACIER, June 8.

I DICTATE the eighth dispatch from Camp Three. I say dictate, as I am unable to write, as I am just recovering from an acute attack of snow-blindness.

Above towers Everest, powdered with fresh snow, still and windless and half-shrouded in that type of damp, sticky cloud which surely this time presages the advent of the monsoon proper.

CLIMBERS' FATE.

All Records Broken by Mallory and Irvine.

The fate of Mr. Mallory and Mr. Irvine is dealt with in the following dispatch, dated June 11, from Lieut.-Colonel Norton:

BASE CAMP, June 11.

WITH the deepest regret I add these few lines continuing the above dispatch. Mallory and Irvine perished on the mountain beyond all doubt.

They were last seen by Odell from Camp Six going strong for the top.

THE KING GREETS MR. & MRS. ASQUITH.

THE PRINCE AND HIS DOG.

Few Things Worse than to Lose it.

LIFE POOR WITHOUT ANIMAL FRIENDS.

THE Prince of Wales presided last night at the centenary banquet in the Hotel Cecil of the R.S.P.C.A., of which he is president. In proposing prosperity to the society he said it had been helped materially by Queen Victoria, who was a great lover of animals.

"I think that some of the love of animals has descended to me," he said, amid cheers. "At any rate, I know I have it."

"To me life without horses, dogs and other animal friends would be a poor thing, and I feel that that view is shared by most but not all of the people in this country."

Later he said: "There are very few things worse I can imagine than being very fond of a dog and losing it."

PUPPY DOGS' TAILS.

Mr. John Galsworthy, responding to the toast proposed by the Prince of Wales, said he was told that when the Prince of Wales was at Osborn his Royal Highness declared that when he became King he would abolish sin and would not allow anyone to cut the tails off puppy dogs. (Laughter.)

It was a large order, but by the presence and the words of the Prince that evening they felt he was still of the same mind in regard to the symbolic declaration and that all animals, human and otherwise, would find in him their kindest friend. (Applause.)

A GOLF STORY.

Lord Lambourne said he understood, when the Prince played golf, he was usually accompanied by a terrier, which probably mitigated the language he understood was sometimes used by people who played golf. (Laughter.)

The Prince, in reply, returned thanks for the kind words spoken about him. "But at the same time," he said, "I think you have been ragging me a little to-night. (Laughter.) Lord Lambourne said I take my dog, of which I am very fond, to golf courses, which I am very fond, to golf courses.

10,000
AT
PALACE

ASCOT OU
SPLEND

RADIANT

TALKS TO L
AND THEI

BY NORAH

LONDON'S mo
son culmina
the Royal Garden
the King and Que
of Buckingham P.

Ten thousand g
ing every phase
Colonial life, stro
sunshine on the v
most beautiful p
London." Magni
word to describe

Early arrivals
straight to the h
which border th
North side. By l
quarter of an hou
had opened, ther
in the shade to
guests began to
groups, enlivene
sunshades.

East vied wit
splendours of rai
side with Paris c
Indian women in
turbaned men in l
appeared in stran
the black coats an
English men visit

QUEEN IN H

Just on the stroke
bands of the Royal
the Scots Guards str
he said, "I think
their way across th
The Queen was w
gown of lace and gre

---

the ridge; the black spot moved. Another black spot became apparent and moved up the snow to join the other on the crest. The first then approached the great Rock Step and shortly emerged at the top; the second did likewise. Then the whole fascinating vision vanished, enveloped in cloud once more.

Mallory and Irvine were never seen alive again. Odell reached Camp VI at 2 p.m. to discover another indication of Mallory's absent-mindedness – he had left his flashlight in his tent. Odell climbed a further 60 m (200 ft) in dense cloud, whistling and yodelling in an attempt to guide the pair back to Camp VI in the gloom. However there was no sign of either man. Odell lingered until 4.30 p.m. when, in accordance with Mallory's earlier instructions, he headed back down the mountain. At that stage Odell was not unduly worried, but when field glasses were unable to detect Mallory and Irvine the following morning, he resolved to climb back up to Camp VI, which he reached at midday on the 10th. There he found everything exactly as he had left it two days

Above The *Daily News* reports the Everest tragedy.

previously. It was evident that Mallory and Irvine had not been back. Gallantly Odell pressed on upward, his search becoming ever more desperate in deteriorating conditions. He lamented:

> This upper part of Everest must be indeed the remotest and least hospitable spot on earth, but at no time more emphatically and impressively so than when a darkened atmosphere hides its features and a gale races over its cruel face. And how and when more cruel could it ever seem than when balking one's every step to find one's friends?

By 12 May the party had given up all hope of them returning alive and set off for home. As the climbing world tried to piece together what could have happened, Odell stated that he thought his sighting of the two men had been on the Second Step at 8,596 m (28,200 ft) on the north-east ridge. Since this was believed to be the last major obstacle to be surmounted en route to the summit, Odell concluded that there was "a strong possibility" that they had reached the summit of Everest, only to perish on their descent, either from a fall or sheer exhaustion.

Then in 1933, on another expedition to Everest, an ice-axe, probably Irvine's, was found at about 8,410 m (27,600 ft), some 90 m (300 ft) below the First Step. This discovery, together with descriptions of the 100 ft high Second Step as a formidable obstacle, one which Mallory and Irvine certainly wouldn't have been able to climb in the five minutes during which Odell saw them, led Odell to revise his views. He now believed that he must have seen the two men on the First Step, some 90 m (300 ft) lower down the ridge, and that therefore it was highly unlikely that they had reached the summit. The general consensus of opinion was that one or both men had made a fatal slip during their descent. However the arguments surrounding their disappearance never went away and would be revived spectacularly 75 years after the event.

The 1933 Expedition – Almost There

For the next eight years after the ill-fated 1924 venture, the Tibetan government refused all requests for further Everest expeditions. Then in late August 1932, permission was finally granted. Eager to capitalize on the change of heart, the Everest Committee prepared a party for an attempt the following spring. The most experienced Everest climbers were unavailable but there were plenty of young pretenders willing to test their skills and nerve in the Himalayas. It was decided from the outset to take a large party to offer a wider choice for the final assault. Ten potential summit men, with an average age of 30, would operate under the leadership of 48-year-old Hugh Ruttledge. The years since the previous expedition had witnessed a marked improvement in some of the equipment. A new double-skinned tent offered additional protection against blizzards at lower levels while those at the higher camps benefited from both improved tents and better wind-proof clothing. Another bonus was the introduction of lighter and more efficient oxygen apparatus.

Learning from past mistakes and armed with the new equipment, Ruttledge drew up his plan. The long march across Tibet to reach Everest, which had proved so draining to his predecessors, was to be taken at a more leisurely pace. By arriving in the region earlier, the team would be able to acclimatize gradually. Once Camp IV had been established on the North Col, a greater urgency

Above The party for the 1933
Everest expedition.

would be introduced so that the final assault could be completed before there was any danger from the monsoon, although there was always the risk in late May of the *chhoti barsat*, a short period of unsettled weather, which could convince climbers that the monsoon had arrived early. It was hoped to have two or three assault parties at peak fitness, supported by Sherpas, ready for the final push in the second half of May.

Accordingly, Base Camp was established on 17 April, 12 days earlier than any previous expeditions, and by 6 May, Camp III had been set up at 6,400 m (21,000 ft), at the foot of the North Col. However the slopes up to the North Col had deteriorated in the intervening years and it was another nine days before Camp IV was established on a ledge 75 m (250 ft) below the col, a spot where it was hoped some shelter would be obtained from the biting west winds. It was now that the weather took a hand. A violent storm imprisoned the party there for four days and no sooner had Camp V been established at 7,830 m (25,700 ft) than a three-day blizzard forced a retreat to Camp IV. When the weather finally improved on 28 May, Camp V was re-established and, with a supreme effort the following day, Percy Wyn Harris, Lawrence Wager and Jack Longland set up Camp VI on a small sloping ledge at 8,350 m (27,400 ft). There, Wyn Harris and Wager spent the night of the 29 May, 180 m (600 ft) higher than any previous tent had been pitched.

Meanwhile Longland took the eight porters down, only to be trapped by a sudden blizzard at the top of the north ridge. He had chosen to return by a different, safer route but in the driving snow, it required all his expertise to guide the men back to Camp V. He recalled:

The wind came in terrifying gusts, forcing us to cling or cower against the rocks to avoid being blown bodily away. My snow-goggles soon became useless, choked with snow. I took them off, only to find that eyelids and eyelashes coated up as well … Every 10 minutes I called a halt to count up my band and collect them together, and then with a few shouted words of encouragement in what I hoped was Nepalese, off we pushed again, fighting our way down against the bitterly driving snow.

Back at Camp VI, Wyn Harris and Wager embarked on the first assault. There was still doubt about the best route to the summit. Norton had reached the great couloir in 1924 by means of a diagonal traverse of the yellow rock band below the north-east ridge, but Mallory had opted for the crest of the ridge via the two steps. Knowing how insuperable an obstacle the couloir rocks had been to Norton, Wyn Harris and Wager chose the steps and close to the First Step, Wyn Harris found the ice-axe from Mallory and Irvine's attempt. Mallory's forgotten flashlight was also discovered…in perfect working order. The First Step

Above Plane approaching Everest during the 1933 photographic expedition.

Right First aerial photographs of Everest 1933.

was conquered easily but, head-on, the Second seemed infinitely more formidable. Searching for an alternative route, they lost valuable time and, running out of daylight, were forced to retreat to Camp VI. They had reached the same height as Norton.

Another storm and heavy snowfall wrecked the chances of the next pair, Frank Smythe and Eric Shipton. When they did finally emerge from Camp VI on 1 June, Shipton was too exhausted to proceed, leaving Smythe to soldier on alone. He reached the same point as Norton, Wyn Harris and Wager but, although he had daylight on his side, the previous day's blizzard had made the snow too treacherous to attempt the difficult final 275 m (900 ft) to the summit. Reluctantly, he turned back – so near and yet so far.

The 1934 Expedition – Eccentricity Personified

The late spring of 1934 saw the most audacious attempt yet to climb Everest – a solo venture by Maurice Wilson, the man dubbed "the mad Yorkshireman". The 36-year-old ultimately harboured dreams of becoming the first man in space. In the meantime, despite a weakened left arm – the result of a First World War wound – he was content to conquer Everest single-handed. He planned to do so by crash-landing a Gypsy Moth, which he had recently bought and named Ever-Wrest, on the lower slopes of the mountain and then climbing to the top. There were to be no arduous treks across Tibet for Wilson. Two slight drawbacks immediately presented themselves – Wilson had never climbed a mountain in his life nor had he ever flown a plane. He remedied the former by taking a holiday in the Lake District and the latter with a course of flying lessons in London. Undeterred by crashing the plane on his way to say goodbye to his parents in Bradford – this caused a three-week delay – or by a telegram from the Air Ministry refusing him permission to fly, he set off for northern India. Against all the odds, he arrived safely but abandoned his plan to land on Everest after being forbidden to fly over Nepal or Tibet. Instead he sold the plane and made for Darjeeling where he studied mysticism and practised living for days without food. He also primed his spirit to survive levels of cold and hardship that would kill a mere mortal. It was, he thought, ideal preparation for his assault on Everest.

Heavily disguised as an Indian, he recruited three Sherpas and headed for the Tibetan border, but at Camp III, with no ropes or practical equipment to sustain such a venture, the porters went on strike and refused to go any further. They tried to dissuade Wilson from proceeding – using both argument and force – but he would not be swayed and set off up the mountain alone, taking with him a tent, three loaves, two tins of oatmeal, a camera, and a silk Union Jack, which he intended planting on the top of Everest. He told the bemused Sherpas to wait two weeks for his return. "You go to death," they called out as he disappeared into the distance but he simply waved back cheerfully and pointed to the summit.

Journeying much of the way by night, he reached the Rongbuk Valley by the middle of April. But his effort was doomed to failure. After nine days, he hadn't even made the top of the East Rongbuk glacier. However he refused to give in and, on 31 May, made his final diary entry before setting off once more. It read: "Off again, gorgeous day". His body was discovered a year later by Charles Warren, a member of the 1935 Everest expedition, lying in the snow at an altitude of

6,400m (21,000ft) in the upper reaches of the East Rongbuk glacier. He had died apparently died from exhaustion and cold while in the act of taking off his boots. Next to his body were his diary, his camera and his Union Jack. His tent had blown away. Over the years, Wilson's equipment has been found at regular intervals by climbers on the glacier – a sad epitaph to a gallant, if foolhardy, individual.

1935 Recce – New Route Discovered

In the spring of 1935, Tibet gave approval for another official expedition covering the year from June 1935 to June 1936, thereby enabling the Everest Committee to despatch a reconnaissance team in 1935 to pave the way for a full-scale expedition the following year. In particular, the reconnaissance party wanted to examine the possibility of another route to the top since by looking again at Everest's western ridge and the unexplored Western Cwm, a vast snow basin dismissed by Mallory in 1921 as "cold and forbidding". And whereas Ruttledge remained adamant that the only time for an assault was between 7 May and 15 June, the reconnaissance proposed to determine whether an assault could be made during the monsoon or immediately after it.

Led by Eric Shipton, the reconnaissance team found that climbing in the monsoon season was definitely too dangerous owing to the constant threat of avalanches. The western ridge was again

Below Camp II on the East
Rongbuk glacier for the
1935 expedition.

deemed impracticable but Shipton thought the Western Cwm looked quite promising. "The route up it did not look impossible," he said, "and I should very much like to have the opportunity one day of exploring it." But to do so would mean establishing a base in Nepal and that country was still a forbidden land.

The 1936 Expedition – Narrow Escape

The 1936 expedition was led by Ruttledge but any hopes of reaching the summit were destroyed by an early monsoon that rendered the North Col highly dangerous. After days confined to their tents, Shipton and Wyn Harris made one last desperate attempt on 5 June but were nearly swept to their deaths by a mighty avalanche. Luckily the avalanche rumbled to a standstill a few yards from the edge of a 120 m (400 ft) drop and the two men were able to scramble to safety. Among the Sherpas on this hapless expedition was a young 19-year-old named Tenzing. Far from becoming disillusioned by the catalogue of misfortunes that befell Ruttledge and his men, the experience whetted Tenzing's appetite for future adventures on the world's highest mountain.

The 1938 Expedition – Monsoon Trouble

As storm clouds gathered over Europe, experienced Himalayan mountaineer Bill Tilman led another Everest expedition in 1938. Favouring the method pioneered by Shipton of taking a small party (seven climbers and 31 porters) and travelling light, Tilman had established Camp III at its traditional position near the foot of the North Col by 26 April. But a succession of illnesses surged through the party, costing valuable time, and by the time they were ready to proceed, on 18 May, it was too late. Another early monsoon had deposited deep snow on Everest. On 8 June, Shipton and Frank Smythe set up Camp VI at 8,291 m (27,200 ft), but the depth of the snow brought significant further progress to a standstill. Two days later, another pair – Tilman and Everest newcomer Peter Lloyd – struck out for the summit but met a similar fate. It was now all too obvious that it was impossible to climb the last 610 m (2000 ft) of the north face with deep snow on the rocks. An early monsoon had wrecked yet another attempt to conquer Everest.

1947 – Echoes of Maurice Wilson

Although the Second World War put a halt to any further organized expeditions, it did not dissuade the occasional romantic from attempting to achieve the impossible dream. One such character was Canadian Earl Denman who in 1947 embarked on an unauthorized solo climb. Taking a leaf out of Maurice Wilson's book, he disguised himself as a Sherpa and crossed Tibet illegally. Perhaps the most remarkable aspect of Denman's jaunt is that he managed to recruit the services of two of the most famous Sherpas of all – Tenzing and Ang Dawa. It was Tenzing's fourth attempt on the mountain and although fully aware that Denman had no permission, no money and precious little experience, he found himself unable to resist the Canadian's overtures. Tenzing later admitted:

> Any man in his right mind would have said no. But I couldn't say no. For in my heart I needed to go, and the pull of Everest was stronger for me than any force on earth.

After nearly being arrested by a Tibetan patrol, the trio trekked to the foot of the North Col but by then they were extremely weak. An added obstacle was that Denman's equipment was woefully inadequate for tackling such terrain and, following a feeble attempt on the col, they had little option but to abort the mission and turn back. When his boots wore out, Denman was obliged to walk part of the way back to Darjeeling with bare feet. The 900-kilometre (600-mile) roundtrip from Darjeeling to Everest and back took them just five weeks on foot.

1951 – Route Through Nepal Discovered

Meanwhile speculation continued as to when Everest might eventually be climbed. In his 1942 book, *Upon That Mountain*, Eric Shipton described mountaineering on the upper part of Everest as "a heavy, lifeless struggle" but predicted that one day it would be conquered. The single event which did most to hasten that day occurred in 1949 when Nepal, traditionally closed to outsiders, finally opened its boundaries to mountaineers. Without this change in attitude from the Nepalese government, Everest would have remained aloof and unclimbed for many more years since the habitual – although unsuccessful – route via Tibet to the north face was also closed to westerners after its religious leader, the Dalai Lama, had received a horoscope warning him to beware of foreigners.

Access to Nepal opened up the south and west faces of Everest although in 1949 this appeared of little benefit. After all, Mallory, albeit from a far-off view, had written off the Western Cwm. Only Shipton saw its possibilities. Whatever the doubts, Nepal's relaxation encouraged a new wave of interest in Everest and in 1950 an Anglo-American team, led by Bill Tilman and Dr. Charles Houston, reconnoitred the Khumbu glacier, the gateway to the Western Cwm and the south-west face of Everest. The centrepiece of the glacier is the notoriously dangerous Khumbu ice-fall. After studying it from a distance, Tilman and Houston felt that for a party to try to climb it would be folly as the ice was too unstable.

Given this evidence, the Himalayan Committee of the Alpine Club and Royal Geographical Society (which had succeeded the Everest Committee) took some persuading before agreeing to a further reconnaissance expedition. They finally relented in the face of enthusiastic campaigning by Michael Ward, a young London doctor and climber, who had acquired aerial shots of the region taken by the RAF at the end of the war. One photograph showed what appeared to be a clear traverse line between the Western Cwm and the South Col; another showed the south-east ridge leading from the South Col to the summit – a route that seemed to have far fewer obstacles than the north-east ridge. Thus, under the leadership of Eric Shipton, a team comprising Michael Ward, Bill Murray, Tom Bourdillon and two New Zealanders – Earle Riddiford and

Opposite The 1951 party negotiate the ice cliffs on the descent into the Hongu basin.

Left The 1951 reconnaissance party: (back) Shipton, Hillary, Riddiford, (front) Bourdillon, Murray and Ward.

former New Zealand Air Force officer and full-time bee-keeper Edmund Hillary – met up in Nepal in August 1951. Despite Ward's photographs, the air was one of hope rather than optimism. "We had little hope of success," admitted Hillary later, "just planning to confirm the impossibility of the route and then to head off exploring in the vast untouched area of mountains to the east and west."

Shipton's Progress and Abominable Evidence

Base camp was established below the Khumbu ice-fall, described by Shipton as "a wild labyrinth of ice-walls, chasms and towers" with hip-deep snow. With the constant fear that the ice on which they were to walk would suddenly collapse, it looked impossible to climb, but the spirits of Shipton and Hillary were raised when they ascended 5,791 m (19,000 ft) up a ridge on the neighbouring mountain of Pumori. The higher they went, the more they could see, not only of the ice-fall, but also of the Western Cwm. It became clear that there was a potential route to the summit of Everest – up the ice-fall, through the cwm, then up the west face of the adjoining mountain, Lhotse, before traversing to the South Col (the depression between Lhotse and Everest) and on to the summit. Shipton described the find of a practicable route from the Western Cwm to the South Col as "most exciting".

Buoyed by their discovery, the team spent the majority of the next month negotiating the one major barrier to success – the ice-fall. The left-hand side was covered by avalanche debris from the west ridge of Everest but a way through the maze of crevasses was eventually found to the right of this. By the end of October, the party had safely reached the top of the ice-fall.

Shipton's expedition progressed to the very lip of the Western Cwm, an area in which man had yet to set foot. Their progress was halted by a giant crevasse, some 90 m (300 ft) wide, but they turned back in the knowledge that they had found the way to climb Everest. "We arrived back in Kathmandu full of hope," wrote Hillary, "only to discover that Swiss expeditions had been granted permission for two attempts in 1952. It is surprising how much we resented this news, as though we were the only ones who had any right to the mountain." All the British could do was wait and hope that the prize would still be up for grabs in 1953.

At face value, the route to the south-west via the Khumbu glacier boasted numerous advantages over the old Rongbuk approach from the north, not least because the most difficult terrain on the northern route was over the later stages at an altitude where energy was at a premium. Conversely, the toughest obstacle on the new route was the ice-fall from around 5,547 m to 6,096 m (18,200 ft to 20,000 ft) – a more modest height at which both mental and physical problems were easier to overcome. Thereafter the route to the summit was relatively straightforward by Himalayan standards.

There was another – equally sensational – development from the Shipton expedition – photographs supposed to prove beyond doubt the existence of the elusive yeti or Abominable Snowman. The half-man, half-ape had been part of Himalayan folklore for centuries and was said by the locals to inhabit the untouched snow-covered mountains. But nobody had produced any firm evidence until Shipton brought back photographs of a huge footprint in the snow over 30 cm

Opposite **The 1951**
reconnaissance team trudge
across the frozen wastes.

(13 inches) long (an ice-axe had been placed alongside to act as a comparison) and of a line of similar footprints stretching into the distance.

On 6 December 1951, *The Times* carried a report of Shipton's find under the headline: FOOTPRINTS OF THE "ABOMINABLE SNOWMAN". In his article, Shipton described how, at 4 p.m. on 8 November, he had stumbled across strange tracks in the snow on the Khumbu glacier. On seeing them, Sherpa Sen Tenzing had immediately pronounced them to be the tracks of yetis. Shipton wrote:

> The tracks were mostly distorted by melting into oval impressions, slightly longer and a good deal broader than those made by our large mountain boots. But here and there, where the snow covering the ice was thin, we came upon a well-preserved impression of the creature's foot. It showed three broad "toes" and a broad "thumb" to the side. What was particularly interesting was that where the tracks crossed a crevasse one could see quite clearly where the creature had jumped and used its toes to secure purchase on the snow on the other side. We followed the tracks for more than a mile down the glacier before we got on to moraine-covered ice.
>
> I have in the past come across many of these strange tracks, in various parts of the Himalaya and in the Karakorum, but I have never found any so well preserved as these. Sen Tenzing claims that two years ago he, together with a large number of other Sherpas, saw a "yeti" at a

Right **Eric Shipton's famous**
yeti footprint. A mountain
boot offers size comparison.

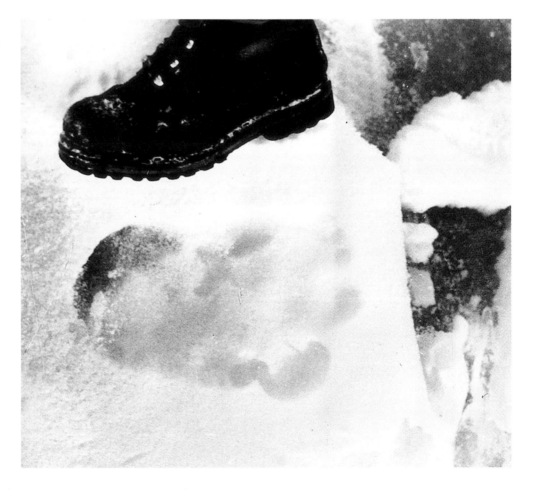

distance of about 25 yards at Tyangbochi. He describes it as half man half beast, about 5 ft 6 in tall, covered with reddish-brown hair, but with a hairless face. Whatever it was that he saw I am convinced of his sincerity. That night as we were settling down to sleep he remarked: "As no one has ever been here before, the yetis will be very frightened tonight by our arrival." I was relieved by this assurance!

As experts examined the prints, the verdicts ranged from a large monkey; an unknown species that was a cross between an ape and a bear; and a practical joke. For Shipton was by no means a conventional figure and was not averse to ridiculing authority. The mystery of the yeti remains.

Another Solo Venture

The opening of Nepal heralded a fresh solo expedition in 1951 when the Dane Klavs Becker Larsen tried to climb the northern pre-war Everest route but via a southern approach. Although his journey was unauthorized, he enlisted a team of four Sherpas, subsequently increasing the number to a dozen. Larsen got as far as the foot of the North Col until his progress was halted by a sudden rockfall. Having never used an ice-axe before, he did not exactly inspire confidence in his porters and they refused to continue, leaving Larsen with no alternative but to abandon the climb.

The 1952 Swiss Expeditions

The Swiss had been trying to stage an Everest expedition since the 1920s so they were determined to make the most of their sudden opportunity and mounted two attempts on the summit of Everest, the first before the 1952 monsoon season, the second after. The first party was 12-strong and the Sherpas were led by Tenzing who had added Norgay ("the fortunate one") to his name. It was his fourth Everest expedition. Proposing to follow the newly discovered Western Cwm route to the top, they established Base Camp on the lower Khumbu glacier on 20 April. The ice-fall, with its continually shifting blocks, lay ahead. The first attempt to climb it ended in failure, but by setting Camp II half-way up and carefully negotiating the avalanche-strewn couloir to the left, nestling under Everest's west ridge, they managed to reach the top on 4 May. After becoming the first humans to set foot on the Western Cwm, they climbed the Lhotse Glacier and moved across to the South Col in readiness for the final push.

On 26 May, Camp VI was duly established on the South Col, but the climb had taken its toll, particularly on the Sherpas. A combination of illness and frostbite had reduced their numbers by three, with the result that their heavy loads had to be carried by the three Swiss climbers in the assault party – Raymond Lambert, René Aubert and Léon Flory. Weighed down with tents, sleeping-bags, oxygen apparatus and food supplies, the climbers made slow progress and it was after dark when they reached the col. Further supplies were brought up but the effort in doing so accounted for three more Sherpas. Now it was just the three Swiss and the redoubtable Tenzing Norgay.

The plan had been to set the highest camp, Camp VII, at a minimum 8,382 m (27,500 ft) on the south-east ridge but, with no back-up, the four men could not cope with heavy loads at that altitude. Instead they set out from Camp VI on the 27th carrying one tent and food for a single day. The weather was clear and the biting wind, which had blighted their stay on the col, had dropped. After being forced to retrace their steps to circumnavigate a steep buttress near the base of the south-east ridge, the men reached a position at just over 8,382 m (27,500 ft). Although they had neither Primus nor sleeping-bags, Tenzing suggested to Lambert that the pair of them spend the night there in the tent before trying for the summit the next day. Flory and Aubert were keen to stay but with only one tent and precious little food, they were left with no option but to return to Camp VI.

"We pitched our tent with great difficulty," recalled Lambert. "The altitude and the wind made our movements awkward. Our legs would not obey us and our brains scarcely functioned. Our hands were more skilful without gloves, but to take them off would cost us dear." They spent a wretched night on the ridge. The wind relentlessly rattled the frail tent and the sheer cold began biting into their bones. Sleep was impossible anyway, but also highly dangerous. To relax the body would be to invite frostbite. With nothing to drink, they melted a chunk of ice over a candle in a tin. It relieved their thirst and kept them awake. They huddled together and playfully shook each other whenever there was a danger of falling asleep. Lambert remembered: "I dared not sleep, must not sleep … In the sky the stars were so brilliant that they filled me with fear."

Incredibly, they possessed the fortitude to start off at six o'clock the following morning but fatigue and bad weather quickly set in. It took them five and a half hours to climb just 198 m (650 ft) of what was far from the most demanding landscape on Everest. They could only manage three steps at a time before stopping for an intake of oxygen. At around 8,600 metres (28,200ft), just 244 metres (800 ft) from the summit, their leaden bodies told them that they could go no further. The climb down was no easier, but they managed to reach the comparative safety of the col by evening. The entire party was now exhausted and, on 1 June, as the wind grew ever fiercer, the climb was finally abandoned.

But the Swiss had the second expedition up their sleeves and on 10 September, a party including Lambert and Dr. Gabriel Chevalley from the first venture, set off from Kathmandu. The Khumbu ice-fall was safer to negotiate at that time of year than in the spring and all went well until they climbed the face of Lhotse on 31 October. Suddenly a huge block of ice broke off from Lhotse's face, crashing down towards six of the party. One Sherpa – Mingma Dorje – was hit on the head and killed and another three were sent tumbling 183 m (600 ft) down into the Western Cwm. One sustained a broken collar bone but all three survived.

The accident shook everyone's confidence. A longer and safer route was reconnoitred up Lhotse, but the delay meant that Camp VIII was not established on the South Col until 19 November. They found the South Col an intimidating place, its barren landscape battered by high winds. A sense of fear had infiltrated the expedition by now and there was a good deal of foreboding about the task ahead. Although an attempt was made to climb the south-east ridge, the weather took a turn for the worse and the party was forced to turn back at around 8,077 m (26,500 ft). They said they could smell death. Everest was still waiting.

Mount Everest expedition team in 1953.

on top of the world

It was a feat comparable to landing on the Moon. Back in 1953, reaching the top of the world was seen as the pinnacle of human achievement and its significance to the British nation was undeniable. For Everest was regarded as a British mountain.

It was named after a Briton and stood like a sentry keeping guard over the northern heights of British India. Eight of the previous unsuccessful expeditions were British and now the latest attempt was led by Colonel John Hunt, one of Montgomery's staff officers and a man whose family had served the Raj for generations. And should it succeed, it would do so in coronation year. For a people still emerging from the shadows of the Second World War, it represented a tantalizing prospect.

Below Colonel John Hunt photographed in front of a map of the Himalayas.

Hunt had received a telegram on 11 September 1952, inviting him to lead the British expedition to Everest scheduled for the following spring. It had come as something of a surprise, since Eric Shipton had originally been appointed leader, but his prejudice against large expeditions and what was perceived in some quarters as a lack of organizational skill prompted a change of heart from the committee. With a new southern route to explore, this was an irresistible challenge for Hunt in spite of the belief in some minds that because so many climbers had got to within 305 m (1,000 ft) of the summit, there was some mystic force protecting the peak itself from human invasion. However, that was just part of the magic of Everest.

Hunt set about interviewing his team, mindful of his own disappointment 16 years earlier when, after being chosen to climb Everest with Ruttledge in 1936, he was subsequently rejected by the Medical Board. "In whittling down the short list to its final proportions," he later wrote, "I was looking for four qualifications. They were those of age, temperament, experience, physique; and I wanted a team every member of which would be a potential 'summiter'." Hunt insisted on meeting candidates personally unless he knew them anyway, so some climbers from overseas who were unable to travel to Britain for the interview had to be passed over. An exception was New Zealander Edmund Hillary, who had been with Shipton in 1951 and was well-known to others whose place in Hunt's team was assured. In fact, Hillary had seriously considered withdrawing from the expedition on hearing that Shipton had been replaced as leader, but Shipton persuaded him to transfer his allegiance to Hunt.

Hunt eventually submitted a list of ten climbers, plus an expedition doctor Michael Ward, mountain physiologist Griffith Pugh and photographer Tom Stobart. The ten were: Charles Evans, 33, a Liverpool surgeon who had been on three previous Himalayan expeditions; Tom Bourdillon, 28, a physicist who had accompanied Shipton on two earlier missions; Alfred Gregory, 39, a Blackpool travel agent who had joined Shipton's 1952 expedition to another Himalayan peak,

Left Shipton's expedition of 1952 to the Himalayan peak of Cho Oyu.

Right Hillary on the summit of Cho Oyu 20,800 ft above Nangra La, 5 May 1952.

Cho Oyu. Apart from 42-year-old Hunt, he was the oldest member of the climbing party; George Lowe, a 28-year-old New Zealand teacher, another member of the Cho Oyu team and an exceptional ice climber; Charles Wylie, 32, a serving officer with the Gurkhas and a former Japanese prisoner of war; Michael Westmacott, 27, an experienced Alpine climber; George Band, the youngest of the party at 23, a tall, bespectacled studious man and former President of the Cambridge University Mountaineering Club; Wilfrid Noyce, 34, a schoolmaster and one of Britain's foremost young mountaineers; Edmund Hillary, the lanky 33-year-old bee-keeper; and Hunt himself. Hunt was only too aware that the total came to an unlucky 13 and was relieved when he was later able to add the name of Tenzing Norgay to the climbing party. Tenzing's participation had been in doubt as he was still suffering from the after-effects of the Swiss expedition. But while convalescing, he wrote to Hunt offering his services although he did not expect to be involved much beyond the ice-fall.

Having selected his team, Hunt considered the qualities required for a successful expedition. He knew that it was essential to allow time for a period of training before the actual ascent on Everest in order for the party to become accustomed to the altitude and equipment. One of the great problems to be overcome in tackling a peak of Everest's magnitude was the rarefied air surrounding the upper part of the mountain, a factor that could render movement virtually impossible, even on relatively straightforward terrain. So acclimatization was vital. Then there was the question of timing. Although the Swiss had found the ice-fall easier in the autumn, winter conditions in the Himalayas were bleak. And of course from early to mid-June there was the monsoon season to contend with, depositing heavy new snow on the mountain and greatly hindering climbing progress. So it was essential to be in position to make the push for the summit during the short period of good weather leading up to the start of the monsoon. The favoured time remained from the middle of May onwards.

It was also important to avoid spending more time on the mountain than was necessary. Earlier parties had suffered not only from the increasing lethargy which takes effect high on the mountain, but also from the strain and tedium of the task lower down. Hunt calculated that they should be prepared to make two, or if necessary, three attempts on the summit, each attempt

Above **The peaks of Everest rising above the clouds.**

backed by material and men. This was where the Swiss had foundered. Thus the equipment, including oxygen supplies, needed to be light and the men thoroughly trained. And above all, Hunt believed that a successful attempt required a large party of 34 Sherpas. Of these, 14 would work in the Khumbu ice-fall carrying loads up to the lip of the Western Cwm; another 14 would ferry the loads up the Cwm to a camp which was to form the Advance Base; and the other six would accompany each assault in pairs from Advance Base to the South Col and onwards and upwards to the summit.

Food was another important consideration. Earlier Everest expeditions had tended to rely on rice, potatoes, eggs, meat and local produce. The bulk foods from Europe had proved too repetitive after weeks on the mountain while the local delicacies had been a taste that many had failed to acquire. Therefore it was thought that the general fitness of the 1953 party would be enhanced by conforming to a European diet, hence more use was made of tinned or vacuum-packed foods. Vacuum-packing had the added benefit of making the rations lighter in weight and less bulky, thus easing the Sherpas' loads. To incorporate the required variety, it was decided to include five luxury boxes to be opened in the later stages of the climb. The contents of these luxury boxes were to be decided by the climbers themselves on the basis of what they would most like to eat at great altitude. For a study of previous expeditions had shown that tastes changed in the rarefied air and climbers began to develop strange cravings. High up on Everest in

1933, Shipton had a sudden yearning for a dozen eggs while Frank Smythe wanted frankfurters and sauerkraut; in 1924 Howard Somervell's favourite diet had been strawberry jam and condensed milk; and on Cho Oyu, Hillary craved pineapple cubes while Campbell Secord longed for tinned salmon. The luxury boxes for 1953 included sardines, chutney, onion flakes, Marmite, 165 packets of assorted soups and cans of pears, apricots and, of course, pineapple.

Fearing the possibility of avalanches on the face of Lhotse, Hunt also borrowed from the Army a two-inch mortar, the bang from which, he thought, would dislodge any lurking avalanches for miles around. Two .22 rifles were later added to the inventory to acquire fresh game for the party.

Hunt was in no doubt as to the most formidable physical obstacle to be overcome. It was the Khumbu ice-fall. "It is in a constant state of activity and change," he said. "Crevasses appear on a hitherto smooth surface overnight. They widen or close with startling suddenness. Great masses of ice, many tons in weight, are at one moment of time poised precariously above the void; at the next they crash downwards, obliterating all in their path, bestrewing the slopes with huge boulders of ice." Despite the fact that it had now been ascended three times (once by Shipton's expedition and twice by the Swiss), it remained a major barrier to success, particularly as its character would undoubtedly have changed considerably by May 1953.

Also, there was that final 245 m (800 ft) of uncharted territory. The Swiss had been in sight of an outcrop known as the south summit, at around 8,748 m (28,700 ft), but could not see beyond it. All Hunt's party had to go on were the aerial photographs, which indicated a narrow crest of snow or ice, battered by the westerly wind so that giant mounds of snow leaned ominously over the eastern precipice. Was Everest saving one final unknown challenge for those who dared to venture that far?

Below The temporary base at Thyangboche.

The Journey Begins

After meticulous testing of equipment both in the Alps and closer to home, on 12 February 1953, Colonel Hunt and his party set sail from Britain aboard the S.S. *Stratheden*, bound for India. From there, they flew on to Nepal where they were joined by Hillary whose bees were particularly active at that time of year. In early March in Kathmandu, Hillary met Hunt for the first time and immediately found him to be forthright and personable. Hillary was also introduced to Tenzing and took to his warmth and friendliness. "For a Sherpa," remarked Hillary, "he was tall and strong. I could see why he had been such a successful mountaineer." For his part, Hunt was relieved to find Tenzing almost fully recovered from his ordeal of the previous May.

Having recruited 350 locals to act as coolies and carry the expedition baggage, the party set off on 10 March on the 17-day trek to the monastery of Thyangboche, 3,962 m (13,000 ft) above sea level and from where they could see Everest rising above its neighbours, Nuptse and Lhotse, for the first time. With a temporary base established at Thyangboche, parties of climbers and Sherpas spent the next two weeks in the surrounding hills, getting used to the oxygen apparatus and climbing 6,000 m (20,000 ft) peaks to help adjust to the altitude. But Hunt had a serious worry. Before setting off on these acclimatization exercises, Tom Bourdillon had discovered that no fewer than 15 of the 48 oxygen bottles were "flat", having leaked while being transported. The bottles were to be used during the acclimatization and also during the assault itself. Hunt feared that a second consignment, due within a week or so, might be similarly incomplete, but fortunately a message reached Kathmandu just before departure and the crate of bottles was checked. Hunt was greatly relieved when they arrived intact since the chances of obtaining replacements from England in time would have been slim.

Hunt was also concerned about the Khumbu ice-fall and felt it imperative that more time must be devoted to a thorough reconnaissance and preparation of a route up it, so that precious days wouldn't be sacrificed later on. Accordingly, during the second part of the stay at Thyangboche, Hunt selected a party, led by Hillary and including George Lowe, George Band and Michael Westmacott, to explore the ice-fall. With no snow forecast, Hillary's coolies, among them a number of women, were not issued with special boots or goggles so an unexpected snowfall reduced them to a sorry state. Those who were suffering from snow-blindness were fitted with makeshift goggles constructed from cardboard, black tape and small pieces of coloured celluloid.

Gamely they pressed on along the Khumbu glacier until they discovered the remnants of Swiss Camp I with its welcome supply of juniper scrub for firewood. Nearby at the foot of the 600-m (2,000-ft) high ice-fall, they established Base Camp on 12 April and the coolies went home. Although hampered by regular afternoon snow and bouts of diarrhoea, which incapacitated Lowe and Westmacott at different times, the team sought out a safe route up the ice-fall through the multitude of crevasses, ice walls and tottering ice pinnacles. For four days, they hacked steps out of the ice to facilitate the passage of the laden Sherpas, wriggled through narrow cracks, fixed ropes and suspended rope ladders as bridges to reach the half-way terrace that had been the perch for Swiss Camp II. Sometimes they would climb up the route in the morning to find that the previous day's tracks had been obliterated by an overnight fall of ice.

Above Checking the climbing equipment for the 1953 expedition.

While Hillary and his men continued carving out a staircase through the upper half of the ice-fall, the rest of the party moved forward to ensure that Base Camp was fully stocked. Camp III was pitched at the top of the ice-fall on 22 April. Hunt found the upper part of the ice-fall every bit as tricky as the lower section. "There was a huge trough," he wrote in his book *The Ascent of Everest*.

It must have measured at least 18 m (60 ft) wide, partly filled with chunks of bare ice, and with a narrow platform some 6 m (20 ft) down, which had sunk from the level of the terrace on which we stood … The exit was perhaps the most dangerous part of the whole journey between Base Camp and the Cwm, for the steep slope on the far side of this trough was covered by blocks of ice of all sizes, piled in indescribable confusion on a wide frontage and extending over some 60 m (200 ft) up the slope. The collapse of any one of these would have spelt disaster to a party below.

For his part, Hillary described it as "exciting climbing and always underneath we had a feeling of tension and danger."

Above **Camp Equipment.**
Left **Breakfast at Thyangboche.**

Onwards and Upwards

Hunt's party was thus at the top of the ice-fall 12 days earlier than the Swiss had been and, equally importantly for what lay ahead, was better acclimatized. A 5 metre (16 ft) wide crevasse which had opened up on the lip of the Western Cwm threatened progress but an aluminium ladder bridged the gap and Hillary, Tenzing, Hunt and Charles Evans set off to choose a site for Camp IV, the Advance Base, near the head of the Cwm. There was a nasty moment when a young Sherpa, Pasang Dorji, plunged into the crevasse and Evans had to use all his strength to haul him up on the rope. Although there was still a long way to go, crossing that crevasse was a key moment for Hunt. "It symbolized our entry into the Western Cwm," he wrote later. "The unpleasant fears of operations with complicated ropeways, to which the Swiss had been compelled to resort, vanished. We felt sure we were through."

On and on they forged, dodging numerous crevasses at the lower end of the Cwm. As they made their way along the Cwm, the whole of Lhotse became visible, its rocks covered by a heavy sprinkling of snow. And then in the distance they were able to make out the South Col of Everest. Although it was a long way off, Hunt's joy at seeing the landscape that he had thought so much about back in London made it almost tangible, and it was with great excitement that he returned to Camp III that evening. The next day, after a three-and-a-half hour journey from Camp III, the team discovered the Swiss Camp IV from the previous autumn and plundered its supplies of bacon, cheese, wafer bread, jam, porridge, milk powder and chocolate.

Once a route to Camp IV had been reconnoitred, the task of ferrying supplies along the Cwm began in earnest. Hunt had calculated that a period of around three weeks was needed for lifting stores into the Western Cwm before mounting the bid for the summit. Over the next week, three parties, each comprising seven Sherpas and two climbers, carried loads from the Base Camp up the ice-fall to Camp III, while another party of seven, led by Alf Gregory and Wilfrid Noyce, ferried

Below An aluminium ladder is used to bridge a wide crevasse on the entry to the Western Cwm.

the loads up to Camp IV at 6,460 m (21,200 ft). Daily falls of snow covered the track but by the time Camp IV was firmly established by Hunt, Bourdillon and Evans on 1 May, around 90 loads, each weighing an average of 18 kg (40 lb), had been lifted up the ice-fall and half of these had been moved on to Camp IV via a daily timetable, which ran with almost clockwork precision. This monumental lift was a testimony to the bonding, acclimatization and general preparation to which Hunt had paid so much attention and was all the more remarkable in that it was achieved despite bouts of sickness (Hunt himself had fallen victim to diarrhoea) and a crampon crisis which left a dozen pairs broken beyond repair. Despite an urgent wireless message to the Himalayan Club, replacements were not expected for several weeks.

Among the carriers was a 13-year-old Sherpa boy, Mingma, who never flinched from transporting loads that would have taxed most adults. His biggest problem was language communication and when Griffith Pugh, the physiologist, ordered some essential equipment to be carried up the ice-fall to Camp III, he was horrified to discover that, instead of test tubes, the box contained mango chutney! Pugh's request had become lost in the translation.

This operation was not without real drama, however. On 26 April, while on his way down the ice-fall to Base Camp, Hillary jumped on to one of the large ice "steps" which divided the crevasses. As he landed, the ice collapsed beneath him and sent him hurtling towards a crevasse. Only Tenzing's expertise at holding his colleague on the rope prevented a serious injury.

Whereas other Everest expeditions had piled exhaustion upon exhaustion, Hunt knew the limits of human endurance. The early arrival in the Himalayas had left the party with room to manoeuvre and, with the great lift all but completed, he arranged a three-day break at Lobuje, two-and-a-half hours' journey from Base Camp down the west bank of the Khumbu glacier. It was an opportunity to be reunited with forgotten things like vegetation and wildlife and for all concerned to recharge their batteries.

The rest period for the ferry teams was from 2–5 May, but work did not come to a complete standstill since Hunt, Bourdillon and Evans went ahead to carry out a preliminary reconnaissance of the next major obstacle, the face of Lhotse, some 1,200 m (4,000 ft) in height from the Western Cwm to the South Col. There were two principal aims to this exercise – to find a route as high as possible up Lhotse and to test the two types of oxygen apparatus at higher altitudes than had been possible to date. Since all climbers were to use oxygen from the Advance Base upwards, the reconnaissance was very much a dress rehearsal for the ascent of Everest itself.

Camp IV, situated in a sheltered hollow less than two kilometres from the head of the Western Cwm, offered a perfect view of Lhotse and the problems to be encountered. One of the most significant landmarks was a rib of rock protruding from the face, which came to be known as "the Geneva Spur". This was the route taken by the Swiss in spring 1952 but all around it were steep rocks with no obvious place to pitch a tent. To proceed via the Geneva Spur would make it impossible to establish any form of camp between the Western Cwm and the South Col – a gruelling climb of 1,220 m (4,000 ft). As the Swiss discovered to their cost, a lack of rest at such an altitude drains the last reserves of energy. In Hunt's view, a much more promising route was via the Lhotse glacier, the route taken by the Swiss autumn expedition. It was considerably longer, requiring a lengthy traverse across the top of the Geneva Spur to the South Col, but its chief benefit was that it offered a choice of possible resting-places, thus allowing the ascent of Lhotse

Left **Wilfrid Noyce leading a group of porters to Camp IV in the Western Cwm.**

to be made in two stages. From his view on the distant slopes of Pumori in 1951, Shipton too had favoured the glacial route.

The preliminary reconnaissance reached 6,860 m (22,500 ft) before being forced to turn back by bad weather. Hunt didn't want to waste energy that would be needed for the actual assault. The following day (3 May) the full reconnaissance party – Bourdillon and Evans with Ward and Charles Wylie in support – set up Camp V at 6,700 m (22,000 ft), at the foot of the Lhotse face. After climbing another 275 m (900 ft), Wylie complained that he wasn't getting any oxygen through his apparatus. His oxygen bottle was empty and when his mask was removed, he was distressed for a few moments, gasping in the thin air. But a narrow ledge was in sight and on it were perched the remains of a tent. It was Swiss Camp VI. With Bourdillon in the lead, Wylie managed to struggle up to it and there, at 7,010 m (23,000 ft), they erected Camp VI. The Swiss had left behind valuable supplies in the form of four charged oxygen bottles. Following a night's rest at Camp VI, Bourdillon and Evans pushed on up the mountain but further blizzards caused them to end the reconnaissance at around 7,315 m (24,000 ft).

Progress up Lhotse was slower than anticipated, due to illness and the weather. It was not until 17 May that Lowe and Noyce established Camp VII at 7,315 m (24,000 ft). Meanwhile the ferrying of supplies continued unchecked below so that all supplies for the assault were at Camp IV or higher when Hunt drew up his final plans for the assault. With fatigue beginning to set in, he decided to go for two instead of three successive assaults so that a near failure by the first party could be exploited by the second without the morale-sapping

Above **Without the skill and durability of the Sherpas, the expedition would surely have been doomed to failure.**

Opposite **Tenzing and Hillary prepare for the assault.**

experience of having to retire from the South Col. If the first two assaults proved unsuccessful and a third was needed, he realized that it would take time to prepare for it. The first party were to use the lighter but experimental "closed-circuit" oxygen apparatus while the second team were to carry the more familiar "open-circuit" equipment. The closed-circuit apparatus offered the advantages of speed and greater endurance. (It was hoped that the summit could be reached in one swoop from 915 m (3,000 ft) below an impossibility with the open-circuit equipment, but doubts about its reliability prompted Hunt to mix and match.)

Each assault party would consist of two men, supported by other climbers below. Bourdillon and Evans were to make the first assault – they had proved themselves to be an admirable

working partnership and had mastered the closed-circuit oxygen apparatus. Their main goal was the south summit. Only if the oxygen and the weather were performing favourably and the terrain between the south summit and the summit itself would allow them to reach the top and back within safe limits should they attempt to go all the way. The second pair were Hillary and Tenzing who, in the words of Hunt, "had established their claim beyond any doubt". To conserve the energies of this quartet, most of the hard graft on Lhotse was performed by the other climbers. Ice expert Lowe's descent on 20 May ended an 11-day stint on the face – an extraordinary feat.

Above **Tenzing crampons down an icy pitch on the Lhotse face.**

Making the South Col

With concern growing about food shortages and further oxygen leaks, Hunt was in need of some good news. It arrived on the 21 May when, in a supreme effort, Noyce and Sherpa Annullu swept beyond the Geneva Spur and completed the route across to the South Col at a height of around 7,925 m (26,000 ft). The rest of the party could only watch from below in wonderment as the two black dots made light of such treacherous terrain. That afternoon, Wylie reached Camp VII with nine heavily-laden Sherpas, followed closely by Hillary and the ever-willing Tenzing, a man who earned Hunt's undying admiration for the way he not only organized the other Sherpas but kept their spirits high. He was a born leader.

Right **Noyce (eating) Wylie and Sherpa guide Annullu take a Himalayan breakfast.**

On 22 May, with Hillary and Tenzing leading, Wylie and 14 Sherpas stacked their loads of 14 kg (30 lb) each on the South Col, weighting them down with boulders to prevent the supplies being blown away by the gale-force wind. The skies were now clear, but everyone knew that situation wouldn't last for long, as the first snowfalls of the monsoon could be expected by the end of the month.

It was on 24 May that the first assault party of Bourdillon and Evans, supported by Hunt and two Sherpas – Da Namgyal and Ang Tenzing – reached the South Col. It had been an arduous climb with Hunt, in particular, struggling to keep pace. Unable to climb two steps without stopping for breath, he began to think his part in the summit push was over until it was revealed that his problems were caused by a kink in his oxygen pipe. The apparatus repaired, the party plodded on. They were unable to follow the tracks from two days earlier – these had been erased by the wind, which had given certain parts of the snow a hard crust. Sometimes their feet would sink into the soft snow beneath; on other occasions they would fail to penetrate the crust. It made the simple act of walking unpredictable and exhausting. At other points the climb was at an angle exceeding 45 degrees. As the day wore on, the party slowed to a snail's pace. Every 100 metres, Hunt stopped and excavated a large hole in the snow where they could sit and rest for a while in what passed as comfort on the upper slopes of the Himalayas. At 4 p.m., they paused on a piece of level ground on top of the Geneva Spur. Hunt could see clearly the south summit of Everest, "an elegant snow spire, breathtakingly close yet nearly 3,000 ft above our heads." From below this summit, the south-east ridge descended. Hunt followed the line of the ridge until he saw a shoulder roughly half-way up. It seemed the perfect spot to place the top camp IX the next day.

The final part of their journey on to the South Col took them downhill to the remains of the Swiss camp, marked by skeletons of tents – bare metal poles with just a few shreds of canvas clinging to them defiantly in the wind. It was like a ghost town and unnervingly eerie. With no time to waste before darkness descended, they set about erecting their own tents which had been brought up there on the 22nd. It was a fearful place, made worse by the driving wind. Hunt's oxygen supply had run out and Evans removed his set to make movement easier. It had little effect. As Hunt remarked:

> We were pathetically feeble, far too weak to compete against that fiendish gale. For over an hour we fought and strove with it, playing a diabolical tug-of-war, trying to put up one single tent which can be put up in one or two minutes lower down. All the time the canvas was being snatched from our hands and we were being caught in a tangle of guy ropes.

As they staggered around helplessly, Hunt tripped over a boulder at one point and lay on his face for five minutes, unable to muster the strength to get to his feet. Bourdillon's oxygen supply also ran out and he too slumped to the ground in a state of semi-consciousness. But with a superhuman effort, aided by the arrival of the two Sherpas, they managed to erect the tents.

The plan had been to push on to the south summit – and perhaps beyond – the next day but the previous day's traumas had left everyone exhausted. This was particularly frustrating as the wind dropped on the 25 May to leave a beautiful, clear day – perfect weather for climbing. And all were only too aware that the weather could change any day. Instead the party stayed at the camp, tucking into salami sausage and four tins of honey left by the Swiss. Hunt also found a tin of tunny fish among the Swiss supplies and was later ashamed to admit that he kept it to himself!

Hunt had planned to dump the supplies needed for the top camp at the shoulder on the south-east ridge, around 8,535 m (28,000 ft), but he now realized that one of the Sherpas, Balu, would not be fit enough to continue. So with everything resting on the shoulders of Hunt and the other Sherpa, Da Namgyal, he decided to take the load as far as possible and wait for the second support party of Alf Gregory, Lowe and three Sherpas, who bore a lighter burden, to take it on up the mountain.

First Assault

While Hunt and Da Namgyal were getting ready at the crack of dawn on 26 May, Bourdillon and Evans were about to embark on the first assault. But there was a snag. Evans' oxygen apparatus had developed a fault, delaying their departure by over an hour. In the event, Hunt and the Sherpa set off first, shortly after 7 a.m., each carrying around 20 kg (45 lb) on their back, but it was heavy going and they were soon overtaken by Bourdillon and Evans. After climbing 425 m (1,400 ft) in three hours, Hunt and Da Namgyal arrived at the little tent left by Lambert and Tenzing a year earlier. They were now on their last legs and, at 8,335 m (27,350 ft), decided they could go no further. They found a rock hollow on the crest of the ridge, which was just large enough to accommodate a tent and supplies, set down their loads (tent, food, kerosene, oxygen bottles, candle and matches) and rested before making the long return down to the South Col.

With lighter loads to carry, Bourdillon and Evans had covered their first 400 m (1,300 ft) from the South Col in an hour and a half, reaching the south-east ridge at 8,290 m (27,200 ft) shortly after 9 a.m. If they could maintain that rate of progress, they would hit the south summit in another 90 minutes or so, leaving time for a final glorious push along the unknown ridge to the very top of the world. But once on the ridge, they slowed alarmingly as the hard surface created difficulty in getting a hold with their crampons. Eventually they reached the shoulder, the highest point attained by Lambert and Tenzing, but by now it had started to snow. Pausing on a gentle slope, they decided to fit fresh oxygen canisters. Both men were carrying two canisters, each of which had a life of approximately three and a half hours. They had already been going for just over two and a half hours so there was probably another hour's supply left. Therefore they could have pressed on towards the south summit and made the changeover there but problems had already been encountered on the expedition when a new canister was fitted. The valves had been known to freeze up. Given that worst possible scenario, it was far safer to take a new canister at this lower level, nearer to camp, than at the remote area of the south summit. Additionally, a fresh canister would assure them of another three and a half hours' oxygen.

However, no sooner were the new canisters fitted than Evans again experienced difficulties with his oxygen. Determined not to give up, he followed his partner slowly up towards the south summit. They finally stood on top of the south summit at one o'clock, at a higher point in the world than

anyone had ever climbed before. Although surrounded by clouds, they could make out the final stretch of ridge to the summit. Ever since Shipton had first suggested the possibilities of this route, mountaineers had speculated as to what the ridge to the summit might look like. At this stage, Bourdillon and Evans just wanted it to be easy. Instead, from their view, it appeared narrow and steep with almost a sheer 2,400 m (8,000 ft) drop to the left down into the Western Cwm. Evans calculated that it would take another three hours to get to the summit. Not only would they not have enough oxygen to get to the summit and back to the camp at the South Col, but they would be doing the latter part of the return journey in total darkness. It was clearly not feasible and, albeit with great reluctance, they decided to return to camp and leave the push to the summit to the second assault party of Hillary and Tenzing.

On the way down, Evans, who was bringing up the rear, slipped and hurtled past Bourdillon, dragging the latter off balance. Fortunately Bourdillon was able to plunge his ice-axe, which had been wrenched free, back into the snow and that served to put a brake on the rope, stopping Evans's fall. They got back to Camp VIII at around 4.30 p.m. and, through frost-covered faces which, to Hunt, made them appear "like strangers from another planet", broke the sad news to the rest of the party who thought they might have made it to the very summit of Everest. But all was not lost. Hillary and Tenzing plus their support party had arrived at the camp in preparation for the second assault.

Just when the party needed some good fortune, fate conspired against them. That night at the crowded camp was, according to Hillary, "one of the worst nights I have ever experienced." The wind rose to gale force, the temperature dropped to minus 25 degrees Centigrade and nobody got any sleep. The wind was still howling on the morning of the 27 May. Even the act of venturing outside the tent required considerable nerve. Upward movement was obviously out of the question but Evans and Bourdillon set off down to Camp VII around midday. However Bourdillon was in a bad way and needed help if he were to get down alive. Leaving Hillary with a parting instruction "not to give in if avoidable" and the promise of further reinforcements, Hunt selflessly helped guide Bourdillon to safety.

Hillary and Tenzing Make their Ascent

After a frustrating day confined to camp, Hillary and Tenzing spent another restless night as the tents continued to be battered by the elements. Mercifully, the wind eased around 8 a.m. and they seized the opportunity to think about setting off and establishing the top camp, Camp IX, high on

the south-east ridge. Alas, only one of the three Sherpas – Ang Nyima – was fit for action, so Hillary and Tenzing were left with no choice but to carry their own loads. Lowe, Gregory and Ang Nyima left Camp VIII at 8.45 a.m., carrying over 18 kg (40 lb) apiece. With 23 kg (50 lb) on their backs, Hillary and Tenzing followed on an hour-and-a-quarter later so that they could move swiftly up the steps made by the first group and thus conserve energy and oxygen.

They reached the ridge at midday and moved on up to Hunt's dump. They considered this to be still too low for an effective summit camp and, adding the extra gear to their loads, progressed steadily up the ridge. Within two hours, they were tiring visibly and looking for a suitable ledge on

Above **Hillary and Tenzing** about to leave the South Col to establish Camp IX

which to erect their tent. Since most of the ground was at an angle of 45 degrees this was no easy matter, until Tenzing remembered a spot from the previous year and suggested a traverse over steep slopes to the left. There, they managed to find a sloping ledge under a rocky face – just big enough to take their tent. It wasn't ideal but it was the best site they had seen. Wasting no time, Lowe, Gregory and Ang Nyima dropped their loads and began their journey back to the South Col. Hillary and Tenzing waved them goodbye and watched them disappear into the distance. They then spent the remainder of the daylight hours digging out two small ledges in the snow before pitching the tent precariously across them in readiness for spending the night at 8,500 m (27,900 ft), just over 300 m (1,000 ft) from their goal.

That evening, Hillary and Tenzing dined on dates, sardines on biscuits, jam, honey and tinned apricots thawed out over the Primus. Hillary rested in a half-sitting position, which although not exactly comfortable, at least enabled him to provide the tent with an extra anchor against the frequent

Above **Hillary and Tenzing on the shelf at the top of the Lhotse Face during the second assault.**

Right **Hillary and Tenzing push on towards the summit.**

gusts of wind. They had enough oxygen for four hours each during the night at one litre per minute. Hillary used his in two bursts – from 9–11 p.m. and 1–3 a.m. "While wearing the oxygen we dozed and were reasonably comfortable," he recounted, "but as soon as the supply ran out we began to feel cold and miserable."

The wind eventually eased during the night and Friday 29 May dawned fine. Hillary and Tenzing peered out of the tent at 4 a.m. and began preparing for the biggest day of their lives. A sizeable consumption of lemon juice and sugar – to stave off dehydration – was followed by their last tin of sardines on biscuits. With the Primus cooker roaring away, Hillary took the opportunity to thaw out his climbing boots, which were frozen solid. After hurrying through breakfast, they put on their gear, culminating in three pairs of gloves – silk, woollen and windproof.

At 6.30 a.m., they crawled out of the tent, connected up the oxygen apparatus and set off in the early morning sunshine. Still concerned about his cold feet, Hillary asked Tenzing to lead the way. Far above them, they could see their first objective, the south summit. As Hillary's feet warmed up, he took over in front and they moved slowly but steadily along the ridge. The soft unstable snow made progress on the very top of the ridge particularly treacherous so they descended a little on the steep left side to find a route where the wind had created a thin crest capable of taking their weight. The snow there was only marginally more predictable – suddenly giving way without warning – and it was with some relief that they came up to a tiny hollow and found the two oxygen bottles left there by Bourdillon and Evans during the first assault. Hillary

scraped the ice off the gauges and saw that there was sufficient oxygen to get them back down to the South Col. The steep climb up the last 120 m (400 ft) to the south summit was more arduous than most. There was no alternative route and so the pair had to make the best of it, constantly battling against the peril of the snow beneath their feet suddenly falling away. Higher up the face, the snow was firmer and they were able to chip steps and crampon up to the south summit. It was 9 a.m.

With a mixture of excitement and apprehension, they stared out at the unclimbed ridge that lay between them and the summit of Everest. The sight was as daunting as Bourdillon and Evans had suggested. Especially alarming were the huge overhanging masses of snow and ice, which "stuck out like twisted fingers" over, the 3,000 m (10,000 ft) drop of the east face. If they accidentally set foot on to these cornices, it would spell disaster. The one hope was that the snow between the cornices on the right and the rock precipices on the left appeared to be firm and hard. That being the case, they would be able to cut a trail of steps in it. But, said Hillary, "if the snow proved soft and unstable, our chances of getting along the ridge were few indeed."

Before stepping on to the virgin ridge, Hillary did his oxygen sums and reckoned that they had enough to last another four and a half hours. Then for the moment of truth. To Hillary's intense relief, the snow was indeed crystalline and firm. With two or three rhythmical blows of the ice-axe, they were able to hack out steps of sufficient size to accommodate their boots. A pleasant bonus

was that the ice-axe sank readily into the snow, providing a firm anchor for the rope. Edging towards the west face at one point, Hillary looked down 2,440 m (8,000 ft) to see the minuscule dots of Camp IV on the Western Cwm.

Insulated against the cold by their special high-altitude nylon weatherproof clothing, both men were feeling remarkably well – all the more so after Hillary had removed a few icicles from Tenzing's oxygen mask – and after another hour, they reached the foot of what appeared to be the last major hurdle between themselves and the summit – a 12 m (40 ft) high rock step. As Hillary himself later commented, the rock, smooth and with precious few holds, would have presented little more than an interesting Sunday afternoon problem to a group of climbers in the Lake District, but at such an altitude and with energy and time ebbing away, it was a formidable obstacle and would represent the difference between success and failure. All looked lost until Hillary spotted a narrow crack between the rock and one of the great cornices on the east side.

> I jammed my way into this crack, then kicking backwards with my crampons I sank their spikes deep into the frozen snow behind me and levered myself off the ground. Taking advantage of every little rock hold and all the force of knee, shoulder and arms I could muster, I literally cramponed backwards up the crack, with a fervent prayer that the cornice would remain attached to the rock.

Once at the top, he flopped down in exhaustion. "Lying there panting I felt a glow of triumph – maybe we were going to make it after all." Tenzing duly followed. He never learned to write but instead dictated his account:

> On top of the rock cliff we rested again. Certainly, after the climb up the gap we were both a bit breathless, but after some slow pulls at the oxygen I am feeling fine. I look up; the top is very close now; and my heart thumps with excitement and joy. Then we are on our way again. Climbing again. There are still the cornices on our right and the precipice on our left, but the ridge is now less steep. It is only a row of snowy humps, one beyond the other, one higher than the other. But we are still afraid of the cornices and, instead of following the ridge all the way, cut over to the left, where there is now a long snow slope above the precipice. About a hundred feet below the top we come to the highest bare rocks. There is enough almost level space here for two tents, and I wonder if men will ever camp in this place, so near the summit of the earth. I pick up two small stones and put them in my pocket to bring back to the world below.

As the pair progressed purposefully along the ridge, Hillary's enquiries as to his partner's state of health were met by a cheery smile and a wave. The only bar to success now was monotony. Every step seemed much the same; the ridge appeared endless. Hillary began to wonder how long they could carry on. "Our original zest had now quite gone," he wrote afterwards,

Left The joyous moment:
Tenzing on the summit
of Everest 29 May 1953.

Overleaf Tenzing and Hillary
drinking tea in the Western
Cwm after their successful
ascent of Everest.

and it was turning into a grim struggle. I then realized that the ridge ahead, instead of still monotonously rising, now dropped sharply away, and far below I could see the North Col and the Rongbuk glacier. I looked upwards to see a narrow snow ridge running up to a snowy summit. A few more whacks of the ice-axe in the firm snow and we stood on top – a symmetrical, beautiful snow-cone summit.

Hillary was actually the first to set foot on the summit but, with Tenzing only 2 m (6 ft) behind on the rope which joined them, to all intents and purposes they were together. It was 11.30 a.m. Hillary's initial feeling was one of relief.

Below Sherpa Tenzing visiting the South Kensington factory of Cockade Ltd looking at a ten inch to the mile model of Mount Everest with models of himself and Hillary standing on the summit.

I looked at Tenzing and in spite of the balaclava, goggles and oxygen mask all encrusted with long icicles that concealed his face, there was no disguising his infectious grin of pure delight as he looked all around him. We shook hands and then Tenzing threw his arm around my shoulders and we thumped each other on the back until we were almost breathless.

Having taken the precaution of keeping a loaded camera inside his shirt to keep it warm, Hillary proceeded to take the famous photograph of Tenzing on the summit. Tenzing then buried a bar of chocolate, a packet of biscuits and a few sweets in the snow as a gift to the Gods and Hillary did the same with a small crucifix that Hunt had asked him to take to the top. After 15 minutes on the summit, during which they planted the Union Jack, the Nepalese national flag and the United Nations flag, ate mint cake and looked in vain for any indication that Mallory and Irvine had been there, they began the descent, acutely aware of the need to hurry on in order to reach the reserves of oxygen below the south summit. Every step down seemed a step nearer safety.

They reached their tent of the night before at 2 p.m. Loosened from its moorings, it presented a forlorn sight but they paused only for a drink and a change of oxygen sets before pushing on down towards the South Col. Growing weaker by the minute, they were delighted to be met by George Lowe, carrying hot soup and emergency oxygen, a couple of hundred metres above the South Col camp. Just before reaching the tent, Hillary's oxygen supply ran out. He had certainly cut it fine.

Celebration and Coronation

Further down the mountain, the rest of the party waited eagerly for news. At 2 p.m. on 30 May, shortly after the Indian Wireless News bulletin had told the world that the attempt on Everest had failed, the descending group appeared above Advance Base. To an exhausted John Hunt, they looked dejected. He was sure they must have failed. Then suddenly Lowe jubilantly thrust his ice-axe in the direction of the summit. The mood changed. They had made it!

That evening, amid much celebration, they drank a toast to Eric Shipton, the man whose foresight had helped make it possible. Meanwhile James Morris of *The Times* listened to Hillary's story before starting off for Base Camp so that he could relay the message of triumph back to England in time for the Queen's Coronation on Monday 2 June. The news broke in the papers on the morning of the Coronation. *The Times* editorial eulogized:

> Seldom since Francis Drake brought the Golden Hind to anchor in Plymouth Sound has a British explorer offered to his Sovereign such a tribute of glory as Colonel John Hunt and his men are able to lay at the feet of Queen Elizabeth for her Coronation day ... These men of valour and resolution are representatives and champions of humanity itself. Their warfare is not against flesh and blood but against the eternal hills, against the mighty pinnacles of lonely rock and snow. Their victory is a victory for the human spirit.

A wave of euphoria swept the country. Advertisers were quick to capitalize on the feat. In that same edition of *The Times*, Pye Communications Ltd boasted that "throughout their brilliantly successful expedition the Mount Everest team relied on radio communications equipment supplied by Pye." Telegrams of congratulation from the Queen and British Prime Minister Sir Winston Churchill arrived via the British Ambassador in Kathmandu and, as the party said farewell to Everest and the Khumbu glacier, they were greeted like royalty wherever they went. Tenzing was hailed as a national hero in Nepal and Hillary and Hunt were knighted. Hillary was astonished by the scale of the welcome – he hadn't realized how interested non-mountaineers would be in their achievement. But he took in his stride the fact that he had become public property and always viewed the feat with commendable modesty. Looking back, he said: "I haven't the slightest doubt that we who were attempting Everest in 1953 were the lucky ones. We were not driven by ideas of fame and fortune (or certainly I wasn't). All we wanted to do was climb a mountain that had been a constant challenge for more than thirty years."

FIRST DAY COVER
INDIAN POSTS & TELEGRAPHS

Above **The conquering heroes on their arrival in London and a First Day Cover celebrating the achievement.**

American climber John Evans crosses a crevasse on the Khumbu icefall, by way of a delicate log bridge

3

because it was there

When asked why he had wanted to climb Everest in the first place, George Mallory had replied simply: "Because it is there." And even though the great peak had finally been conquered, there was no shortage of climbers eager to follow in the footsteps of Hillary and Tenzing, just because Everest was there.

The second successful ascent, via that same south-east ridge, took place in May 1956 by a Swiss expedition led by Albert Eggler. Four climbers – Jürg Marmet, Ernst Schmied, Hans-Rudolf von Gunten and Adolf Reist – reached the summit in what came as a belated consolation prize for the Swiss who had come so close in 1952.

Chinese Footsteps

Of course, there were still fresh challenges to be met on Everest, particularly by unconquered routes, the most notable of which remained the North Col route that had defeated so many British expeditions in the inter-war years. In 1960, a massive 214-strong Chinese expedition set up Base Camp on the Rongbuk glacier and began the ascent of the North Col. It took an exhausting five weeks and, after another six days taken to reach the Second Step on the north-east ridge, they were forced to retreat in a state of utter exhaustion. Two weeks later, they started the process of restocking their camps and on 23 May, following a rigorous six-day climb, 13 members of the team attained the top camp at 8,500 m (27,900 ft). Despite eating little food that evening, three of the party made it to the summit the next day, apparently completing the climb in darkness without bottled oxygen.

News of the Chinese claims was greeted with scepticism in the west, suspicion fuelled by the lack of details. Instead the accounts served as little more than propaganda for the Communist party, expedition leader Shih Chan-Chun attributing the success to "the leadership of the Communist party and the unrivalled superiority of the socialist system of our country. Without all this, we, the ordinary workers, peasants and soldiers, could never have succeeded." To heighten the sense of disbelief, it emerged that two of the Chinese said to have reached the summit – Wang Fu-chou and Chu Yin-hua – had each been mountaineers for just two years and that Chu had removed his boots and socks to climb the fearsome Second Step. But when he later showed

American climbers his toe-less feet and no less a figure than Chris Bonington backed the credibility of the Chinese claims, the ascent was officially accepted. Any lingering doubts were probably removed in 1975 when another Chinese expedition, claiming victory by the same route, erected a red tripod on the summit as proof. This was found there four months later by Bonington's British expedition, who had been attacking the peak from the south-west.

The Americans entered the fray in 1963 with a triple ascent orchestrated by Norman Dyhrenfurth. The idea was for two groups to duplicate the approach of Hillary and Tenzing via the South Col and for another to navigate a new route up to the summit via the west ridge then descend by the south-east ridge to complete the first traverse of Everest. As dissent in the ranks broke out amid accusations of preferential treatment for the South Col parties, Dr. Tom Hornbein and mountain guide

Willi Unsoeld became ever more determined to climb the west ridge. The first South Col pair – Jim Whittaker and Sherpa Nawang Gombu – made it to the top on 1 May and three weeks later, Hornbein and Unsoeld reached the summit on the same day as the second South Col team of Luther Jerstad and Barry Bishop.

The key to the Hornbein/Unsoeld success was the traverse from the west ridge on to the north face and the subsequent climb up the steep 600 m (2,000 ft) couloir, which came to be known as the Hornbein Couloir. At 8,500 m (27,900 ft), the ascent up a vertical rock face with no holds became tougher than ever and they were beginning to run out of oxygen and daylight. Momentarily, they considered going back down but, as Hornbein revealed in his book *Everest: the West Ridge*, it was never really a viable option.

Above **Norman Dyhrenfurth.**

Too much labour, too many sleepless nights, and too many dreams had been invested to bring us this far. We couldn't come back for another try next weekend. To go down now, even if we could have, would be descending to a future marked by one huge question: what might have been? It would not be a matter of living with our fellow man, but simply living with ourselves, with the knowledge that we had had more to give.

Left **Right Mr and Mrs Barry Bishop** of Bethesda, Maryland, pose against the Himalayan background during their April reunion on the slopes of Everest. Mr Bishop, a *National Geographic* staff member, was a member of the National Geographic Society American expedition. Mrs Bishop, a teacher had been trekking through the Himalayas and climbed to 6,096 m (20,000 ft) with her husband.

Overleaf 160 km/h (100 mph) winds are not uncommon on the higher reaches of Everest.

because it was there

Above **Three mighty Himalayan peaks: Everest (left) 8,848 m (29,028 ft); Lhotse (centre) 8,501 m (27,890 ft); and Nuptse (right) 7,879 m (25,850 ft).**

Right **The notorious Khumbu icefall – the only route into Everest's Western Cwm.**

Unsoeld's success was achieved at a cost. It was 6.15 p.m. when he and Hornbein eventually reached the summit and they were forced to bivouac in the open that night at around 8,380 m (27,500 ft). They survived the intense cold but afterwards Unsoeld had to have nine frost-bitten toes amputated. Barry Bishop, who bivouacked with them, lost all his toes.

Over the next 12 years, three Japanese parties, an Indian team and an Italian expedition all reached the summit via the now well-trodden path of the south-east ridge. On 26 October 1973, the Japanese duo of Hisahi Ishiguro and Yasuo Kato became the first to set foot on the summit outside May. But tragedy was often close at hand. On 5 April 1970, six Sherpas accompanying a Japanese expedition were killed by an avalanche on the Khumbu ice-fall. Four days later, a seventh Sherpa died at the same spot, the victim of a falling ice-block. And on 9 September

1974, Frenchman Gérard Devouassoux and five Sherpas were killed by an avalanche on the west shoulder of Everest.

The 1970 deaths occurred during preparations for an ambitious scheme to ski down Everest by 37-year-old Japanese skier Yuichiro Miura. With a parachute trailing behind him, he set off on 6 May from a narrow terrace on the South Col at 7,925 m (26,000 ft). As he jumped off, all he could hear was silence. "I am alone in a world without sound," he later wrote in his book *The Man Who Skied Down Everest*. "Because the air is so thin and the wind is at my back, I feel nothing, like a rocket streaking through vacuous space." Speeding down the steep slope, he was under no illusions about the dangers. "In about six seconds my speed should reach between 175 and 200 km/h (110 and 125 mph). I'll have to pull my rip cord before that. My skis can't possibly edge to a stop on this ice. The chute is my only chance." He pulled the rip cord and waited for what seemed like an eternity for the parachute to open. Just as he was starting to despair, he felt the familiar tug but instead of slowing him down to a manageable speed, the opening of the chute had no effect whatsoever. "Is it the wind, or the thinness of the air?" he queried. "There is nothing for the chute to hold. It drags along uselessly behind me."

Desperately trying to put the brakes on by weaving around the slope, Miura hurtled on towards oblivion. After about 30 seconds, he thought all was lost and resigned himself to death. Having rushed down 1,830 m (6,000 ft) in two minutes, his ski suddenly caught on something. It saved his life. As he toppled head over heels, he came to rest in the snow next to a rock. For Miura, it was the great escape.

Japan's First Woman

Above **Junko Tabei**.

The Japanese expedition of May 1975 was notable for setting the first woman on the summit. Junko Tabei had first become fascinated by mountains at the age of 10 when she went on a school trip to a volcano. In 1970, she made the summit of Annapurna III on an all-female expedition, on the strength of which she was invited to join a women's expedition to Everest. Although Japanese custom forbids a woman to leave her husband for any period without his prior consent, he allowed her to join the expedition as long as she first bore him a child. So by the time the expedition set off, Junko was the mother of a two-and-a-half-year-old girl.

The Everest attempt almost ended in disaster when Junko, six other climbers and six Sherpas were injured by an avalanche that descended on Camp II. But they survived, the weather eased and 35-year-old Junko and male Sherpa Ang Tsering succeeded in reaching the summit 12 days later on 16 May, making her the 38th person to get to the top of the world … but more importantly the first woman. She only just achieved that distinction, because a mere 11 days later, 37-year-old Phantog, a Tibetan member of the controversial Chinese North Col expedition, also climbed to the summit. In doing so, she lost three of her toes to frostbite.

So women had conquered Everest, something that the old British Everest Committee had been convinced would never happen. In reply to a 1924 request from a French woman, Anne

Left The 1975 British
expedition tackle the
Western Cwm.

Overleaf Looking up the
Western Cwm on Everest.

Bernard, to join the next expedition, the committee had informed her in no uncertain terms that it was "impossible to contemplate the application of a lady of whatever nationality to take part in a future expedition to Everest. The difficulties would be too great." Fifty-one years on, humble pie was added to the expedition catering list.

By 1975, six expeditions involving members of both sexes (including a 1971 international party where the popular Indian climber Harsh Bahuguna had succumbed to cold and exhaustion) had tried and failed to find a new route to the top via the south-west face. Then in September 1975, a British expedition led by Chris Bonington finally made it. From the Western Cwm, they climbed the Great Central Gully but at 7,925 m (26,000 ft) the way ahead looked barred by the menacing black cliff known as the Rock Band. However Nick Estcourt and Tut Braithwaite managed to find a route by way of a succession of ramps and gullies, enabling Doug Scott and Dougal Haston to make the summit on 24 September.

Loss of Burke

They were able to do so in near-perfect conditions but two days later when it was the turn of 23-year-old Peter Boardman and Sherpa Pertemba, the weather had taken a distinct turn for the worse. The wind had got up and a storm was blowing in. On the way down from the summit, Boardman and Pertemba were amazed to see through the mists the figure of cameraman and climber Mick Burke. He was sitting on the snow a few

Above **Chris Bonington working out logistics on Everest.**

Opposite **Dougal Haston route finding in the icefall on Everest 1975.**

Overleaf **Porters in the Western Cwm on Everest during the 1975 British expedition.**

hundred yards down a gentle slope leading from the summit. Burke congratulated the pair and said that he wanted to film them on a nearby bump on the ridge and to pretend that it was the summit. But Boardman pointed out that the deception would fool nobody because of the Chinese tripod that was standing on the real summit. At that, Burke asked them whether they would go back and join him on the summit but, with the weather threatening to deteriorate further, Boardman was none too keen and so Burke announced that he would go to the summit alone and would meet them back at the south summit. After taking a couple of photos of Burke, Boardman called out, "See you soon" and saw Burke disappearing off towards the summit.

That was the last anyone saw of Mick Burke. Boardman and Pertemba waited patiently at the south summit for almost an hour and a half, huddled next to the rock fighting to keep out the cold. Pertemba had lost all feeling in his toes and fingers. The wind was howling across the ridge. The storm had arrived, reducing visibility to just 3 m (10 ft). By four o'clock, there was still no sign of their colleague. He should have been back at least three-quarters of an hour earlier. Boardman

tossed away his iced-up snow goggles and, clearing the frost from his eyelashes, peered into the gathering gloom along the ridge for any sign of life. It had taken Scott and Haston three hours on a sunny day to reach the safety of Camp VI and now Boardman and Pertemba had only an hour of daylight left. Boardman summed up his mixed emotions:

Below Mick Burke, last
seen alive just below the
summit in 1975.

At 28,700 ft (8,750 m) the boundary between a controlled and an uncontrolled situation is narrow and we had crossed that boundary within minutes – a strong wind and sun shining through clouds had turned into a violent blizzard of driving snow, the early afternoon had drifted into approaching night and our success was turning into tragedy.

Reluctant to abandon Burke until the last possible moment, they agreed to give him another 10 minutes. When this too proved fruitless, they set off down the ridge. From time to time, they looked back in the direction of the south summit, hoping that Burke had merely been delayed. Nothing.

Burke's precise fate will probably never be known. The most likely scenario is that he reached the summit but that on the way back, as the blizzard hit the ridge, he inadvertently trod on one of the lethal snow cornices and plunged to his death down the east face.

Ascents Without Supplementary Oxygen

From the earliest days of Everest expedition, controversy had raged over the benefits of supplementary oxygen and therein lay a new challenge – to be the first to climb the world's highest mountain without using additional oxygen at any time on the expedition, even to aid sleep.

The challenge appealed enormously to Reinhold Messner, a 33-year-old Italian, and 35-year-old Austrian climber Peter Habeler. Messner had climbed most of the tough Alpine routes by the time he was 20 and, with Habeler, had made the fastest ascent of the notorious north face of the Eiger, halving the previous record. In 1975, the pair had climbed Gasherbrum – the 11th highest mountain in the world – without supplementary oxygen and this success prompted them to attach themselves to the 1978 Austrian expedition to Everest led by Wolfgang Nairz, in the hope of repeating the performance on the grandest stage of all.

The two men set off from their South Col camp at 5.30 a.m. on the morning of 8 May, bound for the summit. However, the weather was appalling and the conditions underfoot extremely difficult. As they began the steep climb to the south-east ridge, they sometimes sank up to their hips in the snow, which made progress sluggish despite their light rucksacks. Where possible, they made a detour on to ice-covered rock where the wind had blown away the snow. "We had to concentrate so hard on every foothold and every handhold," said Habeler, "that there was no time left to think about our exhaustion."

After four hours, they arrived at the top camp. Habeler was acutely aware that they had reached approximately the same altitude as Mallory and Irvine. This sense of history and foreboding began to weigh heavily on his shoulders. Death loomed large in his thoughts for he knew that they were completely alone up there and that no rescue team would be able to assist them in the event of an accident. Messner too had misgivings and wondered whether it was possible even to continue. With no sleeping-bags to enable them to rest there until the weather improved, they decided to press on. There seemed little hope of making the summit but even to get to the south summit without bottled oxygen would represent a considerable achievement. Messner wrote:

> Regularly, after a few steps, we propped ourselves on our axes and, with mouths wide open, gasping for air, rested thus so that every muscle and fibre could work. Yet I felt I was bursting. Higher up, I even had to lie down in order to be able to continue breathing.

Below Reinhold Messner (left) and Peter Habeler (right) after their epic ascent.

The storm intensified as they reached the south summit and stood above the clouds but, curiously, Habeler's fear of the mountain had dissipated with the clouds. Messner was also more confident that they would now make it to the very top. Too tired to talk, the two men resorted to gestures. Habeler no longer had the urge to go back.

I had been seized by a real sense of euphoria. I felt somehow light and relaxed, and believed that nothing could happen to me. At this altitude the boundaries between life and death are fluid. I wandered along this narrow ridge, and perhaps for a few seconds I had indeed gone beyond the frontier which divides life from death … was physically finished. I was no longer walking of my own free will, but mechanically, like an automaton. I seemed to step outside myself, and had the illusion that another person was walking in my place.

Habeler's out-of-body experience was interrupted by cramp in his fingers, a pain he immediately attributed to the lack of oxygen, but after swift massaging, he was able to push ahead. As the summit grew ever nearer, they were practically crawling, one leg in Tibet, the other in Nepal, totally exhausted yet determined to make it. Finally at 1.15 p.m., they struggled up to the summit. Once on top, Messner sat down and, child-like, dangled his feet over the side. A great calm spread through his body. "I breathed like someone who has run the race of his life and can now rest for ever."

Above **Reinhold Messner on the South Col of Everest.**

There was still the matter of the descent, however. Habeler was impatient to leave, and set off alone, covering the route back to the South Col in just an hour (it had taken them eight hours on the way up) partly by sliding down on his bottom. Messner lingered on the summit, unwilling to depart, before eventually following his partner. Once back at Base Camp two days later, they received confirmation that their exploits had left no sign of brain damage. They had proved that it was possible to climb Everest without supplementary oxygen and live to tell the tale.

Messner Goes it Alone

Opposite **The North East ridge of Everest, with the North Col below on the right.**

Constantly on the lookout for another test of man's powers of endurance and survival, Messner aimed to become the first person to climb Everest solo. Again the attempt would be made without carrying oxygen. In Messner's words it was "one man alone and without technological aid on the highest mountain in the world." It was an irresistible challenge and, to add to it, he wasn't going to repeat the South Col route of two years earlier – this time he was going to tackle Everest from the north, the direction from which so many had failed.

His first attempt, in June 1980, foundered in sodden waist-deep snow, but he waited patiently for the first break in the monsoon and tried again in the middle of August. On his back he carried a 44 kg (97 lb) rucksack containing a small tent, sleeping-bag and mattress, a stove and enough food for seven days. The most dangerous part of the ascent was the climb to the North Col up the steep face where the Sherpas had been swept to their deaths by an avalanche back in 1922. As a solo climber, Messner had to negotiate the assorted crevasses without a rope. Starting off at night from his Advanced Base Camp at 6,400 m (21,000 ft) with only a headlamp to guide the way, he soon fell into an 8 m (25 ft) deep crevasse.

> The sweat froze in my hair and beard, but the anxiety in my bones disappeared the moment I started moving, as I tried to get my crampons out of my rucksack. At each movement, however, the feeling of falling again came over me, a feeling of plunging into an abyss, as if the ground were slowly giving way.

Having extricated himself from that predicament by finding footholds for his feet and thrusting himself upwards, he regained his composure and clambered on up the north ridge, his mind taking in Mallory and Irvine and even that other solo artist, Maurice Wilson. As he pitched camp for that first night at around 7,730 m (25,350 ft), Messner pondered that if Wilson had reached that height, he must surely have gone on to reach the summit. But Messner had underestimated the difficulties ahead. He had planned to take the route via the north-east ridge but, finding it covered in thigh-deep soft snow, was forced to traverse the north face to the Norton Couloir. The detour meant that he only climbed 400 m (1,300 ft) on that second day. His confidence was starting to ebb away.

With time against him, he left behind his tent and most of his equipment in order to make himself lighter for his summit bid the next day. The ploy worked and at shortly after 3 p.m. on 20 August, Messner, almost unexpectedly, came across the familiar Chinese tripod and stood on the summit of Everest for the second time in two years. He felt strangely numb. "I squatted down, feeling as heavy as a stone. I just wanted to rest a while and forget everything. At first there was no relief. I was leached, completely empty."

Below The 1982 British Everest expedition.

The Challenge Thrown Open

By now Everest was attracting almost as many visitors as Disneyland. Ascents were becoming commonplace. On 2 October 1979, German Hannelore Schmatz became the fourth woman to reach the summit and, tragically, a day later the first to die on the mountain when she perished from exposure after being compelled to bivouac on the South Col. The expedition, on which no fewer than eight climbers and five Sherpas made it to the summit, was led by her husband Dr. Gerhard Schmatz.

On 17 February 1980, two Polish climbers – Leszek Cichy and Krzysztof Wielicki – achieved the first winter ascent and three months later a Japanese expedition completed the first full ascent of the north face.

Then in May 1982 occurred one of those baffling events for which Everest has become notorious – the disappearance of British climbers Peter Boardman and Joe Tasker. Chris Bonington had led a party to tackle the summit via the then unconquered north-east ridge with its three stark Pinnacles which point menacingly into the sky at altitudes of between 7,925 and 8,380 m (26,000–27,500 ft).

Climbing without supplementary oxygen, Boardman and Tasker set off for their second attempt on the Pinnacles on 15 May, the first attempt having ended when party member Dick Renshaw suffered a mild stroke. With echoes of Mallory and Irvine, Boardman and Tasker were last seen by Bonington on the distant ridge at 9 p.m. on the 17 May approaching the Second Pinnacle. After that, they just vanished.

Above Joe Tasker and Peter Boardman make their way along the Rongbuk glacier in 1982 on their ill-fated journey towards the summit of Everest.

Above **A sad reminder: the memorial to Peter Boardman and Joe Tasker, lost on Everest in 1982.**

Opposite **A member of the ill-fated 1982 expedition pushing up the North East ridge.**

Ten years later, Boardman's body was found by climbers from Kazakhstan in a sitting position near the Second Pinnacle "looking like he was asleep". And in October 1996 the last piece of the jigsaw was discovered when a Japanese expedition stumbled across the body of Tasker lying face down near the top of the Second Pinnacle. It would seem that, after that last sighting, they bivouacked in a snow hole at around 8,230 m (27,000 ft) and then continued for another 180 m (600 ft) the next morning before deciding that the summit was beyond them. Without bottled oxygen they had already spent three days in the so-called "death zone" above 7,925 m (26,000 ft) at which the body degenerates in the thin air and, realizing the dangers, they dumped their surplus equipment and retreated as quickly as possible. But Boardman could only manage to stagger back to the snow-hole where he died from sheer exhaustion. After probably watching his friend die, Tasker gamely battled on to the top of the Second Pinnacle before his body also gave up.

The one outstanding face of Everest still to be tackled at that stage was the east or Kangshung face. Mallory had dismissed it on his 1921 reconnaissance as being far too difficult, particularly the Kangshung glacier. "It required but little further gazing," he reported,

> to be convinced – to know that almost everywhere the rocks below must be exposed to ice falling from this glacier; that if, elsewhere, it might be possible to climb up, the performance would be too arduous, would take too much time and would lead to no convenient platform that, in short, other men, less wise, might attempt this way if they would, but, emphatically, it was not for us.

Attempts on the Eastern Face

During his ascent of Everest in 1953, Edmund Hillary, in company with George Lowe, had looked down the east face into the Karma valley. It was a spectacular view and Hillary had always hoped that one day he might be able to take a closer look. In 1981, 28 years on, he had his chance when he joined an American expedition led by Dick Blum. But the threat of avalanche (there could be as many as one hundred a day),

because it was there

Left The Kangshung or
east face of Everest seen from
the Kangshung glacier.
Lhotse is on the left.

which had contributed to Mallory's judgement, was never far away and, after overcoming the giant 1,065 m (3,500 ft) high buttress in the centre of the face, the expedition was stopped in its tracks by a mighty avalanche which deposited snow 6 m (20 ft) deep on the glacier. As conditions worsened, burying camps and tents in fresh snow, the climb was aborted at 6,950 m (22,800 ft).

Two years later in 1983, a second American expedition, led by Jim Morrissey, attempted the east face. It was a daunting climb – the toughest on Everest. Even with the experience gleaned from a 1980 reconnaissance and the 1981 expedition plus having the technological benefits of winches to ferry their loads, it took them 28 days just to climb the buttress. And once the near-

Below The Alpenglow lights: the Kangshung at dawn.

because it was there

vertical buttress had been surmounted, there remained another 2,285 m (7,500 ft) of perilous avalanche-ridden snow slopes to cover before reaching the summit via the final stretch of the south-east ridge. Two of the Americans were so worried about avalanches that they pulled out. Others thought long and hard before continuing. Illness and discord were rife. To underline the dangers which existed throughout the climb, three Japanese climbers, going up by way of the south-east ridge, fell to their deaths within sight of the summit just as the Americans were putting six men on top. For the Americans – Lou Reichardt, Kim Momb, Carlos Buhler, George Lowe, Dan Reid and Jay Cassell – it was an awesome achievement to be the first to prove Mallory wrong.

A measure of the difficulty of the ascent is that, at a time when as many as fifty climbers a year were setting foot on the summit of Everest, it was another five years before anyone else successfully negotiated the east face. That man was Oxford-educated Stephen Venables, the only Briton in an American party led by Robert Anderson. The route they took was further south than the 1983 expedition and led up the east face on to the South Col but it was one which still had to deal with a formidable 915 m (3,000 ft) buttress. Furthermore, they were climbing without porters or supplementary oxygen.

After storm-force winds had delayed the summit bid by 24 hours, Venables, Anderson and Ed Webster set off from their South Col camp on 12 May. Still exhausted from a 14-hour trek two days earlier, Anderson and Webster gave up 150 m (500 ft) from the summit. Venables ploughed on, but by the time he reached the top it was 3.40 p.m. The weather and darkness were closing in. Pausing only to place dried flowers on the summit for good luck, he began the treacherous solo descent back to the South Col. His mind flashed back to the hapless Mick Burke who had also wandered back from the summit alone, never to be seen again. The memory of Burke's misfortune made Venables steer well clear of the deadly cornices which overhang the east face and, despite hyperventilating and having to urinate in his pants to keep warm, he survived a night of bivouacking and made it back to camp the next day. In the safety of Kathmandu, he phoned home to his parents in Bath. Too modest to mention his triumph, he simply said he was safe and well. When his father Richard asked him about the climb, he replied:

"Oh, I got to the top. Sorry, I'm running out of money for the phone … goodbye!"

Left The Kangshung face –
the toughest climb on
Everest.

New Ways to Conquer

As more and more people mount assaults on Everest (a record 142 made it to the summit in 2000), the feats have come thick and fast. In 1984, an Australian team with little previous experience of high-altitude climbing became the first to ascend the north face via the whole length of the Norton Couloir. And they did it without additional oxygen. In 1988, Frenchman Jean-Marc Boivin carried a light, steerable parachute called a *parapente* to the summit of Everest and jumped off into thin air. He descended 2,440 m (8,000 ft) in 11 minutes and made a perfect landing on the Western Cwm. In May 1998, 49-year-old Welshman Tom Whittaker, who lost his right foot in a car accident 19 years earlier, became the first amputee to climb to the top of Everest and on 6 May the following year Sherpa Babu Chiri spent a record 21 and a half hours on the summit.

Then in May 2001 American Erik Weihenmayer, who lost his sight at the age of 13, achieved the distinction of being the first blind person to stand on top of the world. His toughest challenge was negotiating the ever-changing terrain of the Khumbu Icefall. He recalled:

Above **French alpine guide Jean-Marc Boivin.**

Right **Erik Weihenmayer, the first blind person to climb Everest.**

Opposite **Weihenmayer negotiating difficult terrain on his route to the summit.**

Sometimes you're walking along and then boom, a crevasse is right there, and three more steps and another one, and then a snow bridge. And vertical up, then a ladder and then a jumbly section.

With the help of his climbing partners shouting helpful descriptions such as "Death fall two feet to your right", Weihenmayer eventually made it to Camp I with only a plunge into a crevasse to show for his struggle. But the climb from Base Camp to Camp I via the icefall took him 13 hours. The expedition leader had allowed for seven. However Weihenmayer soldiered on and fulfilled his dream without further misfortune. He said afterwards, "People think because I'm blind, I don't have as much to be afraid of, like if I can't see a 2,000 ft drop-off I won't be scared. That's insane. Death is death, if I can see or not."

Among those joining Weihenmayer on the summit were 64-year-old Sherman Bull, who thus became the oldest person to climb Everest, and his son, Brad Bull. This enabled the Bulls to become the first father and son to summit Everest on the same expedition.

Age was no barrier to scaling Everest and in 2001 Temba Tsheri, a 16-year-old Nepalese schoolboy, became the youngest person ever to reach the top. He had come agonizingly close to

Right **In 2001, 16-year-old Temba Tsheri became the youngest climber ever to reach the summit.**

because it was there

reaching the top as a 15-year-old, only to be forced back within sight of the summit due to a combination of frostbite, exhaustion and deteriorating weather. Before attempting his final push in 2000, he had made the mistake of opening his gloves for some 45 minutes in order to tie his shoes. On returning from the mountain, he had to have five fingers amputated. Happily his 2001 climb passed without incident.

Less fortunate was Michael Matthews who, just turned 23 in May 1999, became the youngest Briton to climb Everest. On making his descent, he disappeared in the face of gales and blinding snow. He was the 162nd person to die on Everest.

In May 1993, Rebecca Stephens, a 31-year-old Kent journalist, achieved the feat of becoming the first British woman to climb "the British mountain". She was part of an expedition following in the footsteps of Hillary and Tenzing to mark the fortieth anniversary of their epic ascent. Stephens, who had only been mountaineering for four years, suffered mounting frustration before finally making it to the top. She and colleague John Barry reached their camp at 7,925 m (26,000 ft) on a calm evening. She recalled:

> The view was straight down the Western Cwm. We could see the complete route from the top of the Khumbu icefall and all the large mountains. We could see the route up to the south summit. We looked up and it all looked very possible.

Above The youngest Briton to climb Everest, Michael Matthews (left), tragically became the 162nd person to die on the mountain.

But just as she was about to make the final assault on 10 May, she was forced to postpone the attempt in order to look after another expedition member – Harry Taylor – whose condition had deteriorated alarmingly after he had reached the summit without supplementary oxygen. It later emerged that Taylor had come within an hour of death. Then violent storms necessitated a further postponement. Their tent was lashed by hurricanes for two nights, the weather being so bad that Stephens and Barry were unable even to build an ice-wall to protect themselves. They had no choice but to descend and wait for the weather to break. A fatal victim of the hurricane – poignantly tragic in view of the date – was Lopsang Tenzing, nephew of Sherpa Tenzing. Lopsang's body was found after he had been stranded in the storm at 7,925 m (26,000 ft) while climbing with an Australian party. Stephens eventually reached the summit on 17 May. Afterwards she said modestly:

> The thing about Everest is that it is not really a technical climb – at least the route we took is not particularly technical. All you need really is endurance and a head for heights.

Of the treacherously narrow ridge leading to the summit, she added:

> I had been warned about the ridge but it was still a bit of a surprise when I actually saw it. I looked down, saw how tiny everything looked and then chose not to look down again!

Stephens was subsequently awarded the MBE for her achievement.

Two years later, another British woman – 33-year-old Alison Hargreaves – wrote her name into the history books as the first woman to reach the summit alone and without additional oxygen. Furthermore, she was only the second person – after Reinhold Messner – to scale Everest unaided via the perilous north ridge. Hargreaves had nurtured the ambition since she began climbing rock faces in the Peak District at the age of 14. She was six months pregnant with son Tom when she became the first British woman to climb the north wall of the Eiger in 1988 and, as a mother of two, she had attempted the Everest

Right Rebecca Stephens pictured with a sherpa during her 1993 bid to become the first British woman to conquer Everest.

ascent in 1994, only to be driven back by freezing winds at 8,382 m (27,500 ft). Conditions were scarcely more favourable this time and she had to make her approach almost along the very top of the north ridge, since the fierce winds had whipped the snow away from the slopes below, leaving treacherous bare rock.

On 13 May, when she knew she was going to make it to the top, Hargreaves burst into tears:

Below **Mountaineer Alison Hargreaves** on her descent from the top of Everest, which she reached on 13 May 1995, unaided and without supplementary oxygen. She was the first woman to achieve the feat.

I was at the summit for 40 minutes, but it felt like five. It was an incredibly emotional experience. I stood there and thought, there is nobody in the world higher than me at this precise moment. It was the best moment of my life.

Alison Hargreaves was not one to rest on her laurels. No sooner had she returned home than she was planning to climb the world's second highest peak, K2. It was just three months later – in August 1995 – that she climbed to the top of K2. On the way down, she was swept to her death by an avalanche.

because it was there

In the Footsteps of History

Another notable Everest ascent was that in 1995 of 35-year-old George Mallory, grandson of ill-fated pioneer George Leigh Mallory. Seventy-one years on, he succeeded on the same route taken by his grandfather. His triumph threw fresh light on the arguments as to whether Mallory and Irvine had managed to reach the top before disappearing. For George Mallory reckoned the infamous Second Step was easy, even in the dark, and added: "I am convinced Mallory and Irvine could have climbed it in 1924."

The debate about the fate of Mallory and Irvine had resurfaced in the 1970s. The Chinese occupation of Tibet had closed the north-east ridge to western mountaineers for many years but when they were able to return and reach the crest of the ridge, they found that the Second Step was by no means as hazardous as it appeared from below. Furthermore, they looked along Noel Odell's sight-path and reported that the Second Step matched his description while the First Step was hardly visible.

In 1979, Wang Hongbao, a Chinese climber assisting a Japanese reconnaissance expedition on Everest, told one of the party that four years previously he had stumbled across the body of an

Above The 1999 Mallory and Irvine Research Expedition.

"old English dead" at 8,100m (26,575ft), a 20 minute-walk from the 1975 Chinese expedition's Camp VI. Although the two climbers spoke in different tongues, Wang was able to convey via hand gestures the message that the dead man's clothes had disintegrated to dust after lying on the mountain for so many years. But before Wang could be questioned further about his find, he was killed the following day in an avalanche.

This tantalizing shred of evidence spurred on the theorists, among them American climber Tom Holzel who concluded that Mallory probably had reached the summit. He suggested that a lack of oxygen may have caused Mallory and Irvine to split up and that the former – the stronger and more experienced climber – had pressed on for the summit while Irvine retreated down the ridge. Both men could have died in separate falls – Mallory near the summit, Irvine at the point where his ice-axe was found. The body spotted by Wang, some 228 m (750 ft) directly below where Irvine's axe had been discovered, was therefore widely assumed to be that of Andrew Irvine.

The riddle captured the imagination of Jochen Hemmleb, a German geology student who began studying photographs from the 1975 Chinese expedition. Observing that the Camp VI from 1975 had been pitched in an entirely different location from most other expeditions' Camp VI, he believed that he could pinpoint the elusive spot and then, by means of a search of the terrain within a 20-minute walk of the camp, uncover the long-lost body of Andrew Irvine.

Hemmleb began publishing his findings on the Internet website EverestNews.com. In the summer of 1998 he received an e-mail from another Everest fanatic, American climber and publisher Larry Johnson. Within a week, the pair were discussing the possibility of joining a commercial expedition to Everest's north face and then branching out to hunt for Irvine. Flicking through brochures, Johnson spotted a trip run by Eric Simonson's Seattle-based International Mountain Guides. It was not a summit climb but one that took clients to 8,000m (26,250ft). Hemmleb and Johnson contacted Simonson, himself a bit-part player in the Mallory and Irvine mystery, having discovered an old oxygen bottle just below the First Step in the course of a 1991 expedition to Everest. Simonson wondered whether it had been left behind by Mallory and Irvine. Won over by Hemmleb's enthusiasm, Simonson recommended that instead of merely tagging on to a commercial expedition, they plan their own thorough search for Mallory and Irvine.

Finding George Mallory

Backed by $300,000 in sponsorship money, the 1999 Mallory and Irvine Research Expedition began to come together. Simonson recruited some of the world's leading mountaineers, including Conrad Anker, Dave Hahn, Andy Politz, Tap Richards and Jake Norton. Not only were they hoping to find Irvine's body but, perhaps even more importantly, the Kodak Vest Pocket camera that had been lent to Mallory and Irvine by Howard Somervell. If they had reached the top, the evidence would surely be on film and encouragingly Kodak technicians had promised that the film, if still intact after 75 years, could probably be developed.

The expedition arrived in Kathmandu on 18 March and by the end of April the camps were in place in readiness for the search to commence. For once the weather was smiling on Everest climbers and with relatively little snow cover, the prospects of finding Irvine's body seemed good. At 5.15 on the morning of 1 May, Politz, Richards, Norton, Hahn and Anker set off from Camp V at 7,800m (25,600ft). They reached Camp VI at 8,200m (26,900ft) around 10.30 a.m. and from there began traversing to the west towards a ridge that Hemmleb had identified as being near to the Chinese camp of 1975. Soon Norton picked up one of the distinctive blue oxygen bottles that the Chinese had used that year. The omens were promising. They were clearly looking in the right area.

As the climbers began to fan out across the north face, Anker started to drift away from the others and to venture slightly further down the mountain. Surveying the terrain before him, he tried to visualise where he would have chosen to pitch camp and concluded that Hemmleb may have erred on the high side. After finding two bodies – both of which were frustratingly recent – Anker glimpsed a piece of blue and yellow fabric flapping in the wind behind a boulder. Investigation revealed it to be nothing more exciting than a shred of modern nylon tent but as he stood there in the late morning scanning the barren mountain, he saw a patch of marble-like white about 30 m(100 ft) away that, to his eyes, was neither rock nor snow. Instinctively he sensed there was something unusual about it, as he described in his book, *The Lost Explorer*:

> I walked closer. I immediately saw a bare foot, sticking into the air, heel up, toes pointed downward. At that moment, I knew I had found a human body. Then, when I got even closer, I could see from the tattered clothing that this wasn't the body of a modern climber. This was somebody very old. It didn't really sink in at first. It was as if everything was in slow motion. Is this a dream? I wondered. Am I really here? But I also thought, This is what we came here to do. This is who we're looking for. This is Sandy Irvine.

Anker alerted the others via radio and gazed at the body that lay before him at around 8,160 m (26,770 ft). The corpse lay face down, frozen into the mountain. His arms were raised and his fingers were planted in the scree, suggesting that he had desperately tried to stop his fall by clinging to the rock face. There were no gloves on his hands and most of the clothing had been ripped from his back and lower torso by the winds of age. He was naturally mummified, the patch of alabaster that Anker had spotted being the immaculately preserved skin of the dead climber's back. A tuft of hair protruded from the leather pilot's cap he was wearing and a hobnailed boot was laced to his right foot. The shoulders and upper arms were covered in the remnants of several layers of clothing – wool, cotton and silk – and a frail white cotton rope was tied to his waist. The rope had broken, indicating that he had been tied to his partner before suffering a major fall. The right elbow appeared dislocated or broken and the right leg was badly broken. The good left leg was crossed over the other as if he wanted to protect it before facing up to an inevitable death on the frozen slopes. As a macabre postscript, there was a large hole in his right buttock through which *goraks* – the big black ravens that frequent the Himalayas – had eaten most of the internal organs.

At first the party looked at the corpse in awe, wary of disturbing it. Then they remembered the purpose of their mission and began hacking at the rock with ice-axes and pocket knives in a bid to excavate the body. In cutting away some clothing, Norton came across a manufacturer's label on the collar of one of the shirts. Beneath it was a name tag that read: "G. Mallory." Why, they

thought, would Andrew Irvine be wearing George Mallory's shirt? Then they found another name tag: G. Leigh Mallory. And then a third. Dave Hahn recalled:

> Then it finally hit us, we had not found Irvine. We had not discovered Wang Hongbao's "Old English Dead" We were in the presence of George Leigh Mallory himself. THE man of the mountain, THE needle in the haystack. Mallory was the man whose boldness and drive we'd grown up in awe of … and now we were touching him. We each then noticed the muscular arms of the climber. Still, after all these years, George Mallory cut an impressive figure.

Wang Hongbao had described a body lying on its side, one cheek pecked out by goraks. This was clearly a different corpse. Therefore Wang must have found Irvine. If so, was he nearby and was he in possession of the much sought-after camera of which there was no sign on Mallory's body?

The search of Mallory's body continued for the next two hours. A pouch around his neck contained a metal tin of bouillon cubes – Brand & Co.'s Savoury Meat Lozenges. With the tin was a brass altimeter missing both its face and hands, and, in an envelope, a perfectly preserved letter from a mysterious woman signing herself "Stella". Innocent though this missive may well be, it sparked rumours that Mallory may have had a secret admirer. Other items emerged from various pockets – a handkerchief monogrammed G.L.M. carefully wrapped around another group of letters, this time from his family; a fingerless glove; a pocket knife; a box of Swan Vestas matches, still in working order; two more handkerchiefs, one wrapped around a tube of petroleum jelly; an assortment of boot laces and straps; adjustable webbing straps attached to a metal spring clip

Above **George Mallory's upper body, showing the patch of marble-like white that first caught Conrad Anker's eye.**

because it was there

(for holding an oxygen mask to the flying helmet); a note from fellow expedition member Geoffrey Bruce; scraps of paper with pencilled gear checklists; and, deep in one pocket, an undamaged pair of snow goggles.

After sealing the artefacts in plastic bags, taking samples of each layer of clothing and a small skin sample for DNA analysis (permission having been granted beforehand by the families of both Mallory and Irvine), the team prepared to give Mallory a decent burial, covering the body with a protective layer of stones so that it would never again be attacked by birds. Finally Politz read Psalm 103 aloud in a brief ceremony. At 3 p.m. they began the descent to Camp V. "It seems an odd thing to say," said Norton later, "but I don't think any of us wanted to leave him. We were very comfortable being with George. He was so impressive to be with, even in death."

Above One of the letters found on Mallory's body.

Having informed the world of their dramatic discovery, the climbers rested at Base Camp before returning up the mountain in the hope of finding Irvine's body and perhaps unlocking some more secrets of the 1924 expedition. In particular Anker was keen to tackle the Second Step without modern equipment in order to ascertain whether it was feasible that Mallory had climbed it within the time scale. On the way they revisited Mallory's body, discovering a wristwatch in a trouser pocket. Cameraman Thom Pollard wanted to take a look at Mallory's face, which was still frozen into the scree. Carefully hacking away at the ice and dirt, he finally came face to face with George Mallory. Pollard recalled:

> The face was in perfect condition. It was ever so slightly distorted by the years of bearing the weight of snow. His eyes were closed. I could still see whiskers on his chin. Over his left eye, there was a hole. There was dried blood, and two pieces of skull sticking out. It was as though someone had taken a ball peen hammer and smashed in his forehead.

Was this the injury that caused, or at least hastened, Mallory's death?

In the meantime the Second Step beckoned. Approaching the First Step – close to where the ice-axe had been found in 1933 – Richards and Norton chanced upon an old oxygen bottle. It was subsequently identified by Hemmleb as being from the 1924 expedition and proved conclusively that Mallory and Irvine at least reached a point just short of the First Step. Anker duly conquered the Second Step – but not without difficulty – and he and Hahn pressed on to the summit. Anker's experiences led him to conclude that it was unlikely that Mallory and Irvine had reached the summit of Everest back on that June day in 1924.

The discovery of Mallory's body and its position shed new light on the probable fate of himself and Irvine. The fact that Mallory's snow goggles were in his pocket suggests that he was descending in poor visibility, or even at night. The snapped rope indicates that, at the critical moment, he had been roped to Irvine. The relatively mild nature of Mallory's injuries show that the pair did not fall from high up on the deadly northeast ridge, but from a spot well down the face of

Left Mallory's broken right leg lay alongside remnants of his clothing.

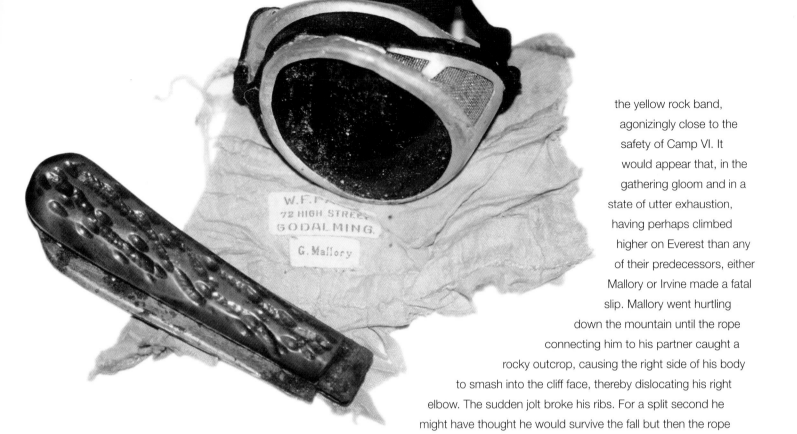

the yellow rock band, agonizingly close to the safety of Camp VI. It would appear that, in the gathering gloom and in a state of utter exhaustion, having perhaps climbed higher on Everest than any of their predecessors, either Mallory or Irvine made a fatal slip. Mallory went hurtling down the mountain until the rope connecting him to his partner caught a rocky outcrop, causing the right side of his body to smash into the cliff face, thereby dislocating his right elbow. The sudden jolt broke his ribs. For a split second he might have thought he would survive the fall but then the rope snapped and he plummeted further towards oblivion. After landing awkwardly on a steep slope, breaking his right leg in the process, he finally managed to arrest his descent by swinging his body around and digging his fingers into the frozen scree. In doing so, he must have smashed his forehead into a shard of rock. He was undoubtedly still alive when he came to rest but was also in great pain. His final instinctive act was to cross his good leg over the broken one. After that, it must be hoped that the end was mercifully swift.

The stunned Irvine may have started to search for his friend but when that proved fruitless he probably attempted to drag himself to Camp VI. Eventually exhaustion and pain overtook Irvine and he surrendered quietly to the mountain. Wang Hongbao's description of the body he found in 1975 stated that it was sitting against a rock, as if asleep. Irvine may have fallen into a sleep from which he never woke.

In 2001 Eric Simonson led a second Mallory and Irvine Research Expedition, but it found neither the camera nor any trace of Irvine. However climbers Brent Okita and Jake Norton did discover Mallory and Irvine's Camp VI and were thus able for the first time to pinpoint its exact location on the northeast ridge. At 8,140m (26,700ft), it was lower on the mountain than previously believed, which meant that Mallory and Irvine had farther to go on their summit day than anyone thought. On the other hand, it meant that they were making better time than was suspected when they were spotted high on the ridge by Noel Odell.

However, without finding the camera, neither research expedition could ascertain whether Mallory and Irvine reached the summit of Everest 29 years before Hillary and Tenzing. Everyone has their own view but many questions remain unanswered. Everest does not give up its secrets lightly.

The Fiftieth Anniversary Climb

Filming a documentary that will air internationally in 2003 – the fiftieth anniversary of the first successful ascent of Everest – a National Geographic expedition led by Pete Athans reached the summit in May 2002. Among its numbers were three sons of Everest pioneers – Peter Hillary (son of Sir Edmund), Jamling Norgay (son of Sherpa Tenzing Norgay), and Brent Bishop, son of Barry Bishop, who was part of the first American team to climb Everest.

Although Jamling Norgay remained at Base Camp to coordinate the team's communications, Peter Hillary and Brent Bishop were involved in the final push. The idea had been to head for the summit in two groups – one following Sir Edmund Hillary and Tenzing Norgay's original route along the South Col, the other climbing the West Ridge, as had two members of Barry Bishop's 1963 expedition. However threatening weather forced the climbers to abandon the West Ridge route in favour of the South Col.

Following a series of frustrating delays for the weather – at one point the team had to turn back after being pinned against the mountain by strong winds – they eventually reached the summit on 25 May. That day was by common consent the last opportunity for a summit push before escalating winds would make any such effort too hazardous. Peter Hillary said:

> The expedition really had some great commonality with what my father and Tenzing faced – summiting with a last-ditch effort at the end of the season. When we went up, there had been lots of fresh snow. At one stage Pete Athans was out in front and it looked like he was breaststroking. He was just scooping snow with his hands and I thought, "We're not gonna make it with these conditions." It was a tough trip but with a great finale and we got some footage of the drops on either side of the ridge near the summit. It's better not to think about it too much because if you fall up there, you fall into different countries.

The ongoing legend of Mallory and Irvine ensures that familiarity with the highest mountain in the world does not breed lack of respect. Despite improved equipment and the high success rate, it is still one of the most dangerous places on earth. As recently as 10 May 1996, eight climbers died in a single day on Everest at the height of a savage storm that threatened to rip everyone from the mountain. In total 15 climbers perished on Everest that year and it is estimated that scattered about the frozen wastes are the corpses of 120 climbers, a grim legacy of years of endeavour on such treacherous terrain. It is an unwelcome reminder that on Everest, success and glory may lie up ahead but death can be just around the corner. As Eric Simonson says:

> George Mallory and Andrew Irvine were the first in what has become a very long list of people who went too far, past the point of no return, and paid the big price.

INDEX

PICTURE CREDITS

The publishers would like to thank the following sources for their kind permission to
reproduce the pictures in this book:

Alpine Club Photo Library, London: 22, 24.
Chris Bonington Picture Library: /Pete Boardman: 94tr; /Chris Bonington: 81tr, 86, 90, 94bl, 97, 98, 100-101, 105tr; /Leo Dickinson: 95, 96; /Jim Duff: 92-93; /Nick Estcourt: 87; /Adrian Gordon: 100; /Dick Renshaw: 99; /Doug Scott: 91.
Corbis: /Johnck Didrick: 108br, 109; /Warren Morgan: 8-9; /John Noble: 88-89; /Galen Rowell: 82-83; /UPI: 62br, 81bl, 84.
Getty Images: /Butch Adams: 42-43; /Hulton Archive: 20; /Chris Noble: 124-125.
ImageState: 6-7.
John Frost Historical Newspapers: 27.
Mary Evans Picture Library: 10tl, 30tl, 30br.
Mountain Camera Picture Library: /John Cleare: 78-79, 85; /Steve Venables: 102-103, 104-105, 106-107.
National Geographic Channels International: National Geographic Channel presents *Surviving Everest*/Photograph: Chris Tait/© NGCI: 123.
PA Photos: 77, 111, 112-113, 114; /EPA: 25, 110.
Rex Features: /Ms. Erin Copland: 115, 116, 119, 120, 121, 122.
Royal Geographical Society: 10cr, 10bl, 11t, 11b, 12, 13t, 13b, 14-15, 16, 17tr, 17bl, 18, 23, 26bl, 29, 33, 34, 36-37, 37br, 39, 41, 49, 50-51, 52, 53, 54, 55tr, 57, 60, 61, 63, 65, 67, 69, 71, 74; /George Band: 72-73; /L. V. Bryant: 32; /Alfred Gregory: 46-47, 55bl, 56, 58, 68, 70; /Indian Airforce: 66; /Lowe: 62tl; /Eric Shipton: 40.
Topham Picturepoint: 19, 26tl, 48, 76, 80, 108tl; /Associated Press: 75.

Every effort has been made to acknowledge correctly and contact the source and/or copyright holder of each
picture, and Carlton Publishing Group apologises for any unintentional errors or omissions which will be
corrected in future editions of this book.

BIBLIOGRAPHY

Abode of Snow – Kenneth Mason (Diadem Books, 1987)
The Ascent of Everest – John Hunt (Hodder and Stoughton, 1953)
Everest – ed. Peter Gillman (Little, Brown, 1993)
Everest, Impossible Victory – Peter Habeler (Arlington, 1979)
Everest: the West Ridge – Tom Hornbein (Sierra Club, 1965)
George Mallory – David Robertson (Faber & Faber, 1999)
Ghosts of Everest – Jochen Hemmleb, Larry A. Johnson & Eric R. Simonson (Macmillan, 1999)
The Lost Explorer: Finding Mallory on Mount Everest – Conrad Anker & David Roberts (Robinson, 2000)
The Man Who Skied Down Everest – Yuichiro Miura with Eric Perlman (Harper & Row, 1978)
To The Top Of The World – Reinhold Messner (Crowood Press, 1992)
Upon That Mountain – Eric Shipton (Hodder and Stoughton, 1943)